mountain bike rides

in & around

The North & South Downs

First published in 2007 by:

Rough Ride Guide Ltd
Walnut Tree Offices
The Old Road
Pishill
Henley-on-Thames
Oxon
RG9 6HS

ISBN 978-0-9548829-4-5

Printed by
Stephens & George Print Group
in the UK

The maps in this book have been
reproduced by permission of
Ordnance Survey on behalf of the
Controller of Her Majesty's
Stationery Office, © Crown
Copyright 100037674.

DISCLAIMER

Mountain biking is a dangerous and addictive
sport. The authors and publishers take no
responsibility for accident, injury, death, loss of
friends, or inconvenience sustained by any user
of this guide as a result of information or advice
contained within this guide.

This book provides information on routes with a
personal insight, but is not necessarily proof of
the existence of a right of way, and does not guar-
antee the safety and well being of any user using
the information or advice contained in this guide.

Ride safely, within your limits and wear a helmet.
RRG accepts no responsibility for any breakage
to you or your bike, getting lost, injured, tired,
lost, hungry, wet, grumpy, sunburnt, cold, or lost.

mountain bike rides in & around **The North & South Downs**

SPECIAL THANKS TO:

My wife Sarah who has inspired and supported me throughout.

My mum for helping finance it.

Friends & family for their help and support.

The riders, clubs and bike shops who have shared with us, their favourite trails.

You for buying this book – I hope you have some great rides.

EDITORS
Max Darkins
Richard Sanders

DESIGNER
Kate Lester
Lee Bainbrigge

PHOTOGRAPHS
Max Darkins
Richard Sanders
Sarah Darkins
Ken Williams
Specialized
Rocky Mountain

TECHNICAL STUFF
Ken Williams aka Mr Grey

foreword by the author

Since the release of the first A4 Rough Ride Guide books we've been lucky to have received lots of really positive feedback from riders. It also made us aware of the need for a smaller, cheaper version of the book - same concept and quality, but not such a big cash outlay. With the option to 'mix n match' further sections into your book through our website, we feel that we have come up with a truly unique product that we hope you enjoy using as much as we did making it.

The North & South Downs offer a great variety of riding - from the legendary pine forest single track of surrey, to the fast chalky South Downs Way in the south, there are a lot of quality trails to keep you busy.

In these A5 guidebooks we've tried to provide information on nearby train stations and how to get to the start of the ride. If trains really aren't feasible, try to share lifts, its far more sociable and an easy way to reduce your collective carbon footprint.

Whether you're simply searching for more local rides or are using this book as a guide on your holiday, I hope that you have some great rides and new experiences, and don't stop telling us what you think.

We now have a 'notice board' on our website which we will use to provide up-to-date news and information on the routes e.g. conditions, changes, etc.
The success of this 'notice board' will rely heavily on your input, so please e-mail us with any news and information you have.

Mountain bikers are generally a friendly bunch, who will stop and chat, admire each others bikes and assist with breakdowns, so lets keep it that way. It is a sport that anyone can enjoy, so make the effort to make everyone feel welcome, whatever their age, sex or ability.

Happy riding.

Max Darkins

INTRODUCTION

The Rough Ride Guide books are designed to let *you* choose which sections you would like to have in your book. The standard book has a selection of routes, to which you can add more routes and further supplements, such as our maintenance & repair manual. These can all be purchased from our website www.roughrideguide.co.uk.

TOP TIP: We advice all riders, especially new comers to the sport, to get the 'Introduction to mountain biking' as it has lots of useful information and tips, to enable you to get and make the most of the sport, and gain maximum enjoyment.

THE ROUTE GRADING

Please bear in mind that peoples opinions vary, as well as their speed and line choice, which all play a big factor in determining the difficulty level of a route. Grading our routes is also made more difficult by the fact that our routes usually have shortcut and extension options, which is why our routes usually have a grading between 2 levels.

We have graded our the routes from Easy to Extreme, bearing in mind the terrain, distance, height gained, and opportunity to bail-out, or be rescued should naything go wrong.

Also, to keep some consistency and familiarity to grading trails, we have adopted the ratings and colour coding used by various parties, including the Forestry Commission (but our yellow is their green).

EASY (YELLOW): Suitable for beginners. Generally wide, well surfaced, easy going tracks.

MEDIUM (BLUE): Suitable for intermediate riders. Rougher terrain, single track, requires a choice of line and some technical ability.

HARD (RED): Suitable for experienced riders only. Good bike control required, quick decision making, and some healthy lungs.

EXTREME (BLACK): Suitable for very experienced and competent riders. Contains some very technical and potentially dangerous terrain.

COUNTRYSIDE CODE

Only ride on open trails
Be in control of your bike at all times
Slow down or stop and let people pass by
Warn people of your presence by calling or ringing a bell, pass slowly and be polite
Don't scare any animals
Don't leave any rubbish
Look ahead and be aware
Be kind & courteous to other trail users
Shut gates behind you

TOP TIP: Fix a bell to your bike to politely warn others of your presence - it has even been known to raise a smile from walkers.

BLOCKED TRAILS
There are a couple of very useful websites provided by the CTC that enable you to report / enter the details of a blocked Right of Way e.g. a locked gate at www.clearthattrail.org.uk or for pot holes in roads (a big cause of cycling accidents) at www.fillthathole.org.uk.

▪ **NOTE:** You are perfectly within your rights to continue along the path (or where it should be), by passing around or climbing over the obstacle.

▪ **NOTE:** If an aggressive animal e.g. a dog is stopping you from progressing on a public ROW, inform the police.

USING ROUGH RIDE GUIDE MAPS

Our aim when producing these guidebooks has been to offer clear, fun and challenging routes, suitable for all abilities. To achieve this we have used the best mapping, sought local riders knowledge, and provided shortcut and extension options. This will ensure that everyone can find and ride the best trails, with minimum effort and hassle.

▪ NOTE: We have made every effort to ensure that these routes only use legal paths, but access rights can change or mistakes be made, so if you are ever unsure, please walk your bike to avoid confrontation.

(RRG) ABBREVIATIONS

To reduce the amount of text you have to read through, we have abbreviated the frequently used words. It looks a long list, but most are obvious.

L = Left
R = Right
SA = Straight ahead / across
Bear = A bend of less than 90 degrees
T-J = T-Junction (usually at 180 degrees)
Fork = Track splits into two directions
X-rds = Cross roads (4 road junction)
X-tracks = As X-rds, but tracks not roads
DH = Downhill
UH = Uphill
FP = Footpath
BW = Bridleway
ByW = By-Way
(P)ROW = (Public) Right of way
RUPP = Road used as public path
BOAT = By-way open to all traffic
DT = Double track (wide enough for a car)
ST = Single track (narrow trail).

▪ NOTE: Emboldened directions provide the 'must know' information, and the other directions provide greater detail for when you may be unsure.

DISTANCE

The (blue) main route is usually around 30 kilometres / 20 miles, which will be suitable for most competent and fit mountain bikers, with (yellow) shortcut and (red) extension options for riders wanting to adjust the length to suit their needs.

HEIGHT

The main route shows the distance and amount of climbing. The extension or shortcut will have a + or - figure, to show the change in distance and climbing from the main route. For example, if the main route is 30 kilometres with 500 metres of climbing, and you ride this and the extension which reads +7 kilometress and +150 meters of climbing, you will ride a total of 37 kilometres with 650 metres of climbing.

TOP TIP: A bike computer is very useful to show you exactly how far you have gone, so you can follow the distances we provide between points. Discrepancies do occur, so use them as a guide, not gospel.

NOTE: The amount of climbing involved on the
▪route is just as important as the distance. Generally, 300+ meters of climbing over 15 kilometres is strenuous, so any ride of 45 kilometres and over 900 meters of climbing is going to be very tough. See the route profile below.

We have provided distances in both kilometres, and miles (in brackets), as although we are starting to become familiar with KM, most of us have grown up using and thinking in miles.

ROUTE PROFILE

These are at the bottom of the route directions, showing you the cross section / height gained and lost, on the main route. The numbers above the profile correlate to the route text numbering.

ORDNANCE SURVEY (LANDRANGER) MAP KEY

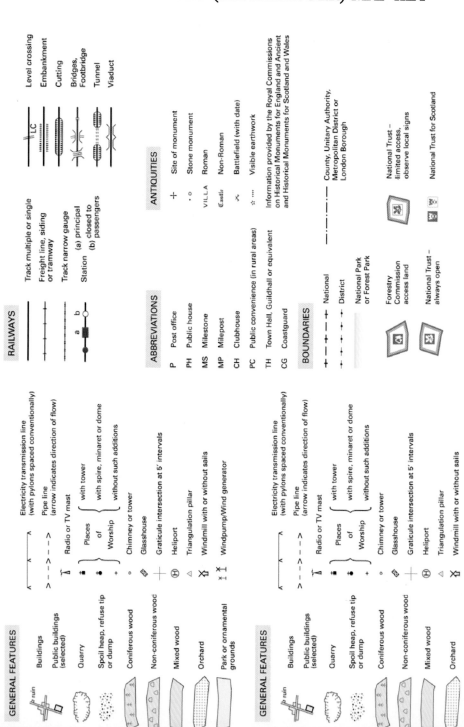

RAILWAYS

- Track multiple or single
- Freight line, siding or tramway
- Track narrow gauge
- Station (a) principal
- (b) closed to passengers

ANTIQUITIES

- + Site of monument
- ∘ Stone monument
- VILLA Roman
- Castle Non-Roman
- ⚔ Battlefield (with date)
- ☆ ···· Visible earthwork

Information provided by the Royal Commissions on Historical Monuments for England and Ancient and Historical Monuments for Scotland and Wales

ABBREVIATIONS

- P Post office
- PH Public house
- MS Milestone
- MP Milepost
- CH Clubhouse
- PC Public convenience (in rural areas)
- TH Town Hall, Guildhall or equivalent
- CG Coastguard

BOUNDARIES

- —+—+— National
- —+—+— District
- National Park or Forest Park
- —·—·— County, Unitary Authority, Metropolitan District or London Borough

- Forestry Commission access land
- National Trust – always open
- National Trust – limited access, observe local signs
- National Trust for Scotland

GENERAL FEATURES

- Buildings
- Public buildings (selected)
- Quarry
- Spoil heap, refuse tip or dump
- Coniferous wood
- Non-coniferous wood
- Mixed wood
- Orchard
- Park or ornamental grounds

- Electricity transmission line (with pylons spaced conventionally)
- Pipe line (arrow indicates direction of flow)
- Radio or TV mast
- Places of Worship with tower
- with spire, minaret or dome
- without such additions
- Chimney or tower
- Glasshouse
- Graticule intersection at 5' intervals
- Heliport
- Triangulation pillar
- Windmill with or without sails
- Windpump/Wind generator

ORDNANCE SURVEY (LANDRANGER) MAP KEY

ROADS AND PATHS
Not necessarily rights of way

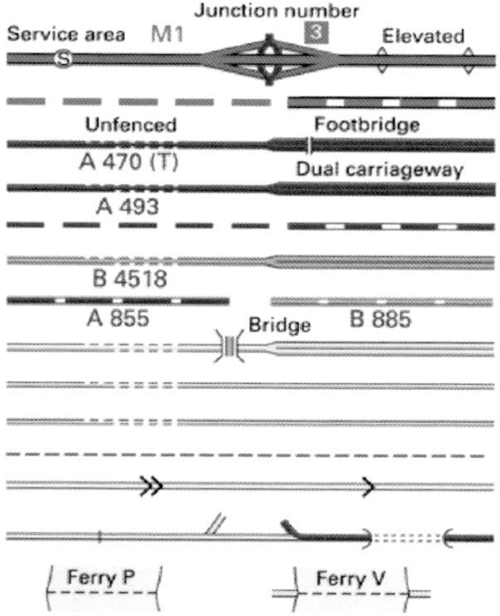

Service area M1 Junction number Elevated

Unfenced A 470 (T) Footbridge

A 493 Dual carriageway

B 4518

A 855 Bridge B 885

Ferry P Ferry V

Motorway (dual carriageway)

Motorway under construction

Trunk road

Main road

Main road under construction

Secondary road

Narrow road with passing places

Road generally more than 4 m wide

Road generally less than 4 m wide

Other road, drive or track

Path

Gradient: steeper than 20% (1 in 5)
14% to 20% (1 in 7 to 1 in 5)

Gates Road Tunnel

Ferry (passenger) Ferry (vehicle)

PUBLIC RIGHTS OF WAY

Footpath ─────────

Bridleway +‑+‑+‑+‑+‑+

Public rights of way shown on this map have been taken from local authority definitive maps and later amendments. The map includes changes notified to Ordnance Survey by (date). The symbols show the defined route so far as the scale of mapping will allow.
Rights of way are not shown on maps of Scotland.

Rights of way are liable to change and may not be clearly defined on the ground. Please check with the relevant local authority for the latest information.

The representation on this map of any other road, track or path is no evidence of the existence of a right of way.

Danger Area Firing and Test Ranges in the area.
Danger! Observe warning notices

OTHER PUBLIC ACCESS

• • • Other route with public access

The exact nature of the rights on these routes and the existence of any restrictions may be checked with the local highway authority. Alignments are based on the best information available. These routes are not shown on maps of Scotland.

♦ National Trail, Long Distance Route, selected Recreational Paths

● National/Regional Cycle Network

─ ─ ─ Surfaced cycle route

4 National Cycle Network number

8 Regional Cycle Network number

ROCK FEATURES

outcrop cliff 650 600 scree

HEIGHTS

50

Contours are at 10 metres vertical interval

· 144 Heights are to the nearest metre above mean sea level

Heights shown close to a triangulation pillar refer to the station height at ground level and not necessarily to the summit.

1 metre = 3.2808 feet

TOURIST INFORMATION

i Information centre, all year/seasonal

Selected places of tourist interest

Viewpoint

P Parking

Youth hostel

Golf course or links

Bus or coach station

⚔ Picnic site

Ă Camp site

Caravan site

Public telephone

Motoring organisation telephone

PC Public convenience (in rural areas)

ROUTES

ROUTES

Numbered unitary areas:
25 READING
26 WOKINGHAM
27 BRACKNELL FOREST
28 WINDSOR AND MAIDENHEAD
29 SLOUGH

No	NAME	GRADING	DISTANCE (KM)	+/- (KM)	CLIMBING (METRES)
01	SWINLEY FOREST	EASY /EXTREME	VARIOUS	VARIOUS	VARIOUS
02	ALTON	MEDIUM	35.7	-16.1 OR +10.3	500
03	CHEESEFOOT HEAD	EASY / HARD	33.8	-20 OR +16.1	545
04	QUEEN ELIZABETH COUNTRY PARK	MEDIUM / HARD	28.2	+10 & +5.8 OR -9.2	745
05	HASLEMERE	HARD	42.8	+7.9	935
06	PUTTENHAM COMMON	MEDIUM	21.5	VARIOUS	375
07	COCKING MAIN	MEDIUM / HARD	28	+13.6	705
08	COCKING SHORT	EASY	12	-	365
09	ARUNDEL	MEDIUM	24.5	-	515
10	WESTCOTT	MEDIUM / HARD	39.4	+2.9 & 3.9	1,000
11	WASHINGTON	MEDIUM / HARD	29.6	-7.3	922
12	DITCHLING MAIN	MEDIUM	18.7	+5.5 & +1.8	495
13	DITCHLING SHORT	EASY	11.2	-	255
14	LEWES	MEDIUM	22	+13.7, +0.65 & +2.8	535
15	FRISTON FOREST	EASY / HARD	30.6	+6.9 & +11.3 OR -14.2	845
16	BEDGEBURY FOREST & BEWL WATER	EASY / MEDIUM	21	+13	290
17	VIGO VILLAGE	MEDIUM	35.3	-10.1 OR +6	665
18	WYE	MEDIUM	27.1	+8.4	535

ROUTE INFORMATION

If you haven't been here before, get yourself along ASAP. Navigation is difficult and you really need some local knowledge, so try and tag along with a group ride, or watch where people go. The sandy ground drains well and there is a choice of technical single track or fire roads so is suitable for all.

This route has some great sections of rooty and stony single track. The climbs and descents are more gradual than steep, which enables the rider to control the difficulty. Not too bad in the wet as it doesn't get over-used......yet.

This ride offers a wide choice of distances, and isn't too technical so should be suitable for all abilities, and only really gets a hard rating for the extension, which adds some distance, with no real option of bailing out if you get tired. Tough going in the wet and some sections can get quite overgrown.

The ride starts and finishes with the good single track of the Orange way marked trail in the QECP. It then spills out onto some classic South Downs terrain, with the option of a hilly extension. The chalky terrain and exposed tree roots, does mean that this is a ride best done in the dry though.

A tough, but great ride, on some lovely single track, through lots of fantastic woods. This area is often over looked by riders, but it does offer some great riding and superb views and terrain, that you probably wouldn't' expect in Surrey. Harder going in winter, but the trees do well at soaking up the worst.

The route will be suitable for most riders as there aren't any very difficult sections. It can also be cut short, or extended by exploring some of the other trails on offer through the common. This area has a sandy base, so it copes pretty well in wet weather.

A challenging loop, with an extension that offers more blinding descents. If you don't have the legs to include the extension on the main route (many won't) come back and do the extension on it's own.

This route starts with a killer climb, and finishes with a superb descent. For those in the group who still has some energy, pop down the route and ride the extension loop, while the others stop at the pub.

Starting from the beautiful town of Arundel everything starts smoothly, then its time for a big climb. Nope to Houghton Forest is just the start of it, but then the superb 3+km descent is worth it, as is the descent back into Arundel. The ground can get boggy and off-camber roots also spice things up.

With a fantastic network of trails throughout this area, providing (probably) the best riding in the South East, it is a favourite haunt for many riders, for miles around. This does create issues with erosion and conflicts with non-cyclists, so please bear this in mind, go when its dry, be courteous and ride safely.

Starting with some classic South Downs riding, its not long before you are into the first of many superb single track descents, towards Findon. More follow around Cissbury Ring, into Steyning, and off the SDW on the homeward leg, to make this a superb ride. The chalky terrain gets very slippery in the wet.

A fun, hilly ride, with more hills on the extensions if you have the energy (others can wait at the top by the pub/ice cream van) and watch as you climb the infamous Ditchling Hill. Gets slippery when wet.

A nice short route, involving a big descent, a big climb, a spin back along the top, enjoying the view, back to the start/ice cream van. If anyone wants to ride a bit more, look at extension 2 (letter B).

The main route uses some well used and familiar trails, the first extension adds quite a few extra miles along some great hills, while the other 2 extensions, add short sharp fun descents, and tough climbs (2and being up Ditchling Hill road).

The main route is a classic ride, with lots of interest the whole way, including a wonderful section near the coast. Friston Forest also has some nice way marked MTB routes through it, including a family route and a technical single track route (see extension 2). Tough going in the wet.

The circuit around Bewl water offers a nice, easy to navigate ride, but can provide a few challenges when ridden flat out. If you want a longer ride, pop over to Bedgebury Forest where you can do a lap of the family trail, or the more challenging intermediate (single track) trail. There is also a freeride and a skills / play area here. Bewl water is closed to cyclists in the winter, and Bedgebury suffers in the wet.

Starting from Trosley Country Park, there is an exciting drop down to the motorway, before an extension option to visit a short downhill/play area. Lots of different tracks make up the next part of the ride, with some fun sections, before heading back along the NDW. Many sections are hard going in the wet.

This is a well known ride in Kent, as it offers some of the best riding around these parts. It is slow going in the wet, but it is still enjoyable.

mountain bike rides

in and around

the north
and
south
downs

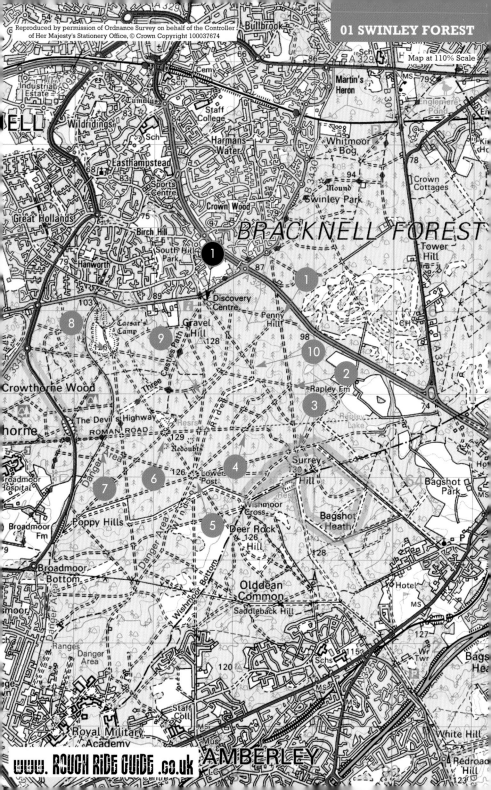

Map at 110% Scale

SWINLEY FOREST
Various

We wouldn't have much luck trying to direct you around Swinley Forest, as there are lots of different (and changing) trails), and you would spend too much of your time looking at the map. Ideally the best way to explore this area is with some local knowledge, so visit www.bobmbc.com for the Berks on Bikes MTB club who do group rides.

Alternatively you can go exploring yourself (and watch where others go), and use this map to find out where you have ended up, as it is very easy to lose your sense of direction in this Forest. There are numbered marker around the forest which we have shown on the map to help you locate your position. There is also a mountain bike specific area (see below for more information) that we have drawn a blue border around, on the map, which has lots of good singletrack.

MOUNTAIN BIKING AREA

The MTB specific area (inside the blue border, marked on the map), has some of the best singletrack. The red posts and arrows around this area will guide you back to marker no.3. A popular singletrack starts by a sandy area, through a small gap into the woods at grid ref: SU 889/636.

There are some jumps, south-west from marker no.3, towards the 'Hydrant'. At the X-rds after about 50 metres, turn left and the jumps are 100 or so metres down here on the right (885/641), but are difficult to see from the track, as they are down in a dip.

The markers

No.	Grid reference
❶	876/660 The Look out
①	885/659
②	887/651
③	887/643
④	881/645
⑤	875/640 (Lower star post)
⑥	871/645
⑦	865/645 (Upper star post)
⑧	864/654
⑨	876/649
⑩	882/653

The names of the forest tracks are as follows:

Bracknell road - between markers 1 & 2
Windsor ride - between markers 1 (via marker 10) past marker 5 and on into the danger area
Pudding hill - between markers 1 & 9
Ladies mile - between markers 6 & 8
Lake Ride - between marker 3 and Rapley lake.
Vicarage lane - track on north-east side of the MTB area
Mill ride - runs parallel on east side of Bracknell road
Devils highway - goes west to Crowthorne from marker 4

OTHER INFORMATION

Cycling (and horse riding) in these woods requires a permit, which costs £1 for the day, and is available at the Look out reception, and Wellington bike hire. For more information contact the 'Look out' reception on tel: 01344 354400.

Berks on bikes (BOB) MTB club have regular rides around here, visit www.bobmbc.com for more information.

▪ **NOTE**: There are some areas that are out of bounds to cyclists, but these are well signposted, and are usually doubletracks, so who cares, just stay off them and ride the singletrack.

TOP TIP: This is a great place to go night riding, but beware that cars often get broken into at the Look Out car park at night, so use alternative options close by.

NON-CYCLING ACTIVITIES:

The Lookout Centre in Swinley Forest, has a hands-on science exhibition, nature trails, children's adventure play park, cafe, and gift shop. For more information, see www.bracknell-forest.gov.uk/lookout.

There is also a Go-Ape (ropes course in the tree tops) see www.goape.co.uk, and just over the road is The Coral Reef swimming pool, (a great place for the kids), see www.bracknell-forest.gov.uk/coralreef for more information.

GETTING THERE: This ride starts from the (free) car park at the Look Out Discovery Centre car park (877/661). This is just off the B3430, west from the roundabout on the A322, just south of Bracknell itself, and is signposted (Lookout / Discovery outpost). Train station at Martin's Heron (Bracknell) - follow the B3430 rd (south) to the 'Look out'.

ACCOMMODATION: B&B's in Crowthorne on: 01344 773876, 750698, 775959 & 772645, Camping in Finchampstead (past Crowthorne) on: 0118 9733928. YHA in Windsor on: 0870 7706096. Bracknell T.I. on: 01344 354409

BIKE SHOPS: Wellington Trek at the Lookout do bike hire, tel: 01344 772797 / 874611. Mountain Trax at the Wyevale Garden Centre, off the B3430 on: 01189 891999, and Berkshire Cycle Co in Crowthorne on: 01344 774529.

REFRESHMENTS: Cafe and toilets at the Discovery centre (car park), so you will never be that far from a cup of tea and slice of cake.

35.7KM (22.2M) 500 metres climbing

❶ START. Exit the car park and turn L for 0.1km (0.05m) then L again on a ByW (SU 671/360). When possible, bear L on the better ST, parallel to the ByW, and keep SA on this for 1m to a driveway. Keep SA past the houses, to a fork and keep SA/L, on a rough track. Bear R then L (effectively SA) on a ST (by the entrance to a stockcar track), along the edge of the woods.

❷ Turn L (effectively SA) on a ST on the RHS of the woods, and follow this, DH, for over 2km (1.25m) to a rd (702/377). Turn L on the rd, which bears R immediately, for 1.2km (0.75m), past a sports centre and hospital, to a T-J (710/385). Turn L on the A339 rd (Beech/Basingstoke) for 0.65km (0.4m) then turn L on a BW (705/388).

❸ Follow this ST on the RHS of the wood, for 1.1km (0.7m) to a fork (697/382) and turn L onto a wider track. Keep SA for 1.4km (0.85m) ignoring any L and R turns, to a DT, and bear R, DH, on this (684/379), for 0.3km (0.2m) to a clearing and keep SA to the rd (685/382).

❹ Go SA, steep UH on a BW, for 0.15m to a fork at the top and bear L on the BW, to a rd (685/389). Turn L on the rd for 0.75m then turn R on a ByW (no SP), opposite a house (676/384). Follow this for 2.2km (1.35m) to a rd/roundabout (663/400) and turn R, or see the shortcut.

❺ After 1km (0.6m) through the village, turn R on a ByW (668/406), DH, for 1.6km (1m), to a minor rd, and keep SA/L to the A339 rd. Turn L on this for 0.1km (0.07m) then turn R on a rd to Shalden (684/411).

❻ UH, for 1.7km (1.05m) to a fork in Shalden and bear R on this rd for 0.1km (0.07m) then L onto a ByW (697/420) opposite the telephone and go DH, to the B3349 rd (707/424) and turn L on this rd or see the extension.

❼ UH, for 0.8km (0.5m) to a X-crds (708/432) and turn L and follow this rd for 4.25km (2.65m), past the gliding club, to the A339 rd (668/438) and turn L on this.

❽ After 0.03km turn R on a BW, UH, into the woods. Keep SA for 2.4km (1.5m) on the main track, which bears L, becoming a ST, to a rd (646/434). Go SA (L then R) on the Three castles BW, for 1.85km (1.15m) to a X-crds and go SA for 0.25km (0.15m) to a (rd) T-J (633/418).

❾ Turn L on the rd for 0.5km (0.3m) into Bradley village, then bear L on a ByW (636/414). UH, for 1.4km (0.85m) to a ByW X-crds (648/409) and go SA on a ByW, DH, to Ashley farm. Bear R to the rd (648/401) and turn L on this for 0.1km then keep SA/R on a ByW, as the rd bears L.

❿ After 1km (0.6m) bear L at a fork (647/391), on the DT, for 1.1 (0.7m) to a 3-way rd junction (655/384) and go SA on the rd. Keep SA after 0.7km (0.45m) as this becomes a ByW.

⓫ UH, past a mast, to a rd (669/374) and go SA on the BW, DH, through the woods, to a X-tracks at the bottom (669/369). Go SA and keep SA for 1km (0.6m), back to the car park entrance (672/361).

SHORTCUT:

-16.1KM (10M) -195 metres climbing

❶ Turn L at the roundabout, for 0.3km (0.2m), past the church, to a X-crds (663/404) and turn L. After 1.6km (1m) on this rd turn L on a ByW (648/400) as the rd bears sharp R (to Ashley farm), and rejoin the route at no.10.

EXTENSION:

+10.3KM (6.4M) +180 metres climbing

❶ Go SA on the ByW, steep UH, to a rd (712/423) and turn R then immediately L, on the ByW. 0.75m to a rd and turn R on this for 0.16km (0.1m) to a X-crds (720/434) and turn L on a ByW. DH, joining a rd after 1km (0.65m), and keep SA for another 1km, then go L on a ByW (719/453).

❷ DH, to a rd and turn L then immediately R on a ByW, UH, for 0.55km (0.35m) to a T-J (711/456) and turn L for 0.4km (0.25m) to a 5-way junction. Go SA on the (RHS) ByW, for 0.65km (0.4m) to the end of the drive, and go SA to some X-tracks at the start of the forest (704/448).

❸ Go SA on the main wide, grassy track through the woods, for 1.7km (1.05m) through a gate to a minor rd/drive (691/439). Go SA on the DT BW, which bears sharp R, DH, in the woods. 0.6m to a fork and keep R, DH, for 1.6km (1m) to a rd (686/464).

❹ Turn L on the rd, for 1.8km (1.1m) to a X-crds (672/454) and go L, for 0.16km (0.1m) then turn R at the fork, to Southrope. 0.55km (0.35m) to a fork in Southrope (671/448) and bear L (Back lane) for 1.2km (0.75m) to a T-J (677/438). Turn R on this rd for 1km (0.6m) to the A339 (668/438), and rejoin the main route at no.8.

GETTING THERE: This ride starts in the (forestry commission) Chawton park wood car park (672/361) near a place called Four marks, nr Alton. Exit the A31 at Four Marks, going north on Boyneswood rd, for 0.4m and go straight ahead/right to the car park, as the rd bears left.

ACCOMMODATION: B&B in Lower Farringdon on: 01420 587076, B&B in East Worldham on: 01420 82392. No campsites or YHAs close by. Alton T.I. on: 01420 88448.

BIKE SHOPS 1st Gear Cycles in Alton on the High Street, tel: 01420 543 922.

REFRESHMENTS: There are lots of pubs, shops in Alton and pubs in Bentworth, and Golden pot on the main route and also in Southrope on extension 2.

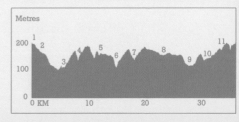

03 CHEESEFOOT HEAD

NOTE: Map at 80%

www. ROUGH RIDE GUIDE .co.uk

33.8KM (21M) 545 metres of climbing

1 START. Turn R on the rd and immediately L on a BW (SDW), 0.1km to a X-rd (SU 527/277) and turn L. Bears L, UH, becoming a DT, to a T-J (530/274) by a big green container. Turn R on the DT, for 0.55km (0.35m) then L on a (easy to miss) BW (530/269).

2 1km (0.6m), DH, to the edge of a wood and turn L on a BW (534/262), UH, past an old yellow container, DH. Keep SA over a track, UH, 1km (0.6m) to a rd (549/256), SA over this, through a gate then immediately R (no SP).

3 After 0.7km (0.45m) bear L at a slight clearing (grassy DT, SA) (546/251) back into the trees. 1km (0.6m), DH, to a rd (548/243) and turn L on this for 1.8km (1.1m) to a X-rds. Go SA on a stony track into the trees, UH, DH, to a big X-rds (563/260) in open, **and go R** or see the shortcut.

4 0.5km (0.3m), UH, to a rd and go SA/R on this for 1km (0.6m) to a T-J. Go R, to a X-rds (569/245) and go L on the rd for 1.2km (0.75m) then R as the rd bears L, to Wind farm (579/241). On SDW, through the farm, for 1.1km (0.7m) to another farm and go L then R, on SDW, to a rd.

5 Keep SA/R on the rd for 0.3km (0.2m) then turn L by the parking area, on a (temporary SDW route for cyclists) BW (598/227). Through 2 gates into a grassy field and turn R shortly on a DT, through a silver gate and then L, DH, on a stoney DT, to a rd (612/233).

6 Turn R on the rd, 1km (0.6m) to a T-J with the main rd in Wanford (621/231). Turn L for 0.15km then L on a rd before the bridge, to Warnford, or see extension.

7 Exit the village after 0.8km (0.5m) and turn L (626/237) on a ROW, SA for 1.95km (1.2m) to a fork. Bear L to a rd and go L on this, then immediately R on ROW (615/252).

8 After 0.65km (0.4m) keep SA/R as join driveway. After 1km (0.65m) turn L on a BW just before a rd (606/ 266). 0.9km (0.55m) to a rd and go SA on the BW, 1km (0.6m) to corner of a rd (589/273), and turn R, to the A272.

9 Go SA for 0.25km (0.15m) then keep SA on the BW as the rd bears L, to a X-tracks (589/283). Go SA, 0.3km (0.2m) to a fork and keep SA/L, to a rd and go SA on the BW. 0.55km (0.35m), under elec. cables, bear L at a fork, for 0.3km, then L again on Wayfarers Walk BW (585/299)

10 DH, along the fields edge, to a rd (580/297) and go SA on the rd opposite (Tichbourne). After 1.3km (0.8m) keep SA on a wide DT BW as the rd bears R into the village, by a farm (571/301).

11 Follow this BW for 2.4km (1.5m) to a T-J and turn R, through a gate and bear L to a (DT) T-J by a barn (555/ 279). Turn R on the DT, to a rd, and go SA on the BW for 1.8km (1.1m) to some X-tracks (537/289).

12 Turn L on the SDW, UH for 1.6km (1m) to A272 rd and turn L, then L again back into the car park (529/277).

SHORTCUT:

-20KM (12.4M) -285 metres of climbing

1 Turn L on the SDW, for 1km (0.6m) past a farm to a rd and go SA, UH, for 0.25km (0.15m), through a gate and turn R (560/271). 0.3km (0.2m) to a T-J (562/272) and turn L, for 1km (0.6m), DH then UH, to a fork by a barn. Keep SA/L to a rd (552/280) and rejoin the route at 12.

EXTENSION:

+16.1KM (10M) 345 metres of climbing

1 Stay on the main rd for another 0.25km (0.15m) then go R on Old Winchester Hill Lane (Clamfield) just over the bridge (625/231). UH for 2.65km (1.65m) to a junction at the top, and go SA/L through a gate on (SDW) BW (645 /216), DH, through silver gate and L on a DT (649/212).

2 To a farm and go L on the drive, to a rd (656/216) and go R on this for 0.5km (0.3m), then L on the SDW (658/ 212). UH for 0.9km (0.55m) to X-rds (666/ 716) and go L on the ByW, 1.6km (1m) DH, to a rd (by Treaton cottage).

3 Turn L on the rd for 0.3km then turn R on a minor rd (Privett) as the rd bears L (670/234). Keep L at a fork after 0.4km (0.25m) for 0.5km (0.3m) to a fork (675/241) and go L. 0.35km to a X-rds and go SA for 0.4km (0.25m) then bear L on a ByW by Old Down farm building (672/250).

4 Through a silver gate, heading towards a yellow house on the grass, to a driveway. Turn R on this, to the A272 rd (663/260) and turn L on this, for 0.65km (0.4m), then go R on a BW (in the lay-by), on LHS of the trees (656/261).

5 UH for 1.4km (0.85m) to a rd (661/273) and go L on this to a main rd and go L on this for 0.15km then R on a ST rd (the drive on the R cuts the rd DH then UH out, but is private). DH, for 0.55km (0.35m) and R at X-rds (651/ 271) UH, on this rd for 2.2km (1.35m) to a fork and go L.

6 0.7km (0.45m), through the village, then L on a DT ByW (no SP) as rd bears R (648/297). Into the woods, DH, on a rocky track with steps, then 1km (0.6m) then L through a single wooden gate (just after BW on R) (639/299).

7 Through another gate and go SA to the other side of the field, and bear R to some X-tracks and turn L into the woods. Keep SA (ST on the R of the DT), to a rd (631/ 291) and turn R on this for 0.5km (0.3m) to a T-J.

8 Turn L for 0.1km then R on a DT (627/294) for 1.3km (0.8m) to a T-J (614/296) (Private sign SA). Turn L for 0.55km (0.35m), exit the wood, to a (ST) T-J (612/ 292) and turn L, (which bears R), for 1.2km (0.75m) to a DT.

9 Turn R on the DT for 0.55km then L on a BW (600/ 289) for 0.7km (0.45m) to another DT (594/287). Turn R on this, to a minor rd and go SA on the BW for 1km (0.6m) (under the elec. lines), then turn L on the Wayfarers Walk BW (585/299), and rejoin the route at no.10.

GETTING THERE: Start from Cheesefoot Head car park, off the A272 - exit the M3 (at junction 9 or 10) and head east on the A31, then R on the A272, for 1 mile then L into the carpark (528/278). Train station in Winchester - follow the South Downs Way signposts.

ACCOMMODATION: B&B in Cheriton at the Flower pots Inn on: 01962 771318, B&B at Milburys pub (on the route) near Beauworth on: 01962 771248, YHA in Winchester on: 0870 7706092, Camping in No Man's Land (near where the A272 leaves the A31) on: 01962 869877. Winchester T.I. on: 01962 840500.

BIKE SHOP: Hargroves cycles in Winchester (on Jewry Street), tel: 01962 860005.

REFRESHMENTS: Pubs on the main route at south of Beauworth, in Warnford, New Cheriton, Cheriton, and Tichborne and on the extension at West Meon.

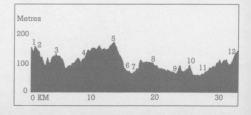

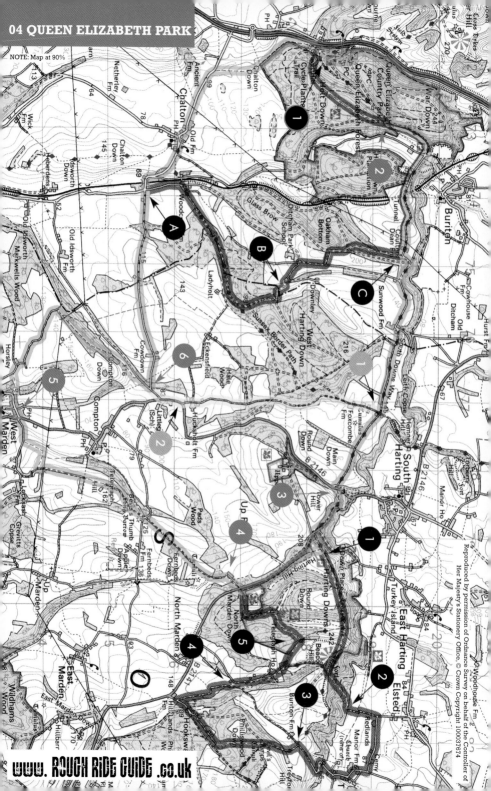

NOTE: Map at 90%

28.2KM (17.5M) 745 metres of climbing

❶ START. From the visitor centre, go to the Woodland area sign (SU 719/185), and turn R, following the orange wooden posts. After 0.4km (0.25m) turn L, UH on a DT, just before a rd and Gravel hill car park just ahead. To a minor rd and turn L on this, then L again at the 2nd orange post, into the woods. Follow the orange markers (parallel to the A3 rd), bearing sharp R, then L, DH across a track, and keep SA, UH to a T-J with a DT (792/192).

❷ Turn L on this DT (South Downs Way) leaving the cycle trail, and keep SA on this DT, bearing R and DH. Go through the car park to the 3-way rd junction (733/198), and go SA on the rd (SDW). Keep SA for 2.8km (1.75m) (changing surfaces) then bear R off the rd, between some buildings, just after a sharp LH bend by Sundown farm (759/193). Follow the SDW for 1.3km (0.8m) to a X-tracks (771/191) and keep SA or see the shortcut.

❸ 1.3km (0.8m) to the B2146 rd, and go SA on the SDW, parallel to rd, for 0.8km (0.5m) then bear L, over the rd (789/181). After 0.25km (0.15m) on Harting Downs, turn R on the BW (791/182) or see extension 1. Follow this BW for 1.4km (0.85m), parallel to the rd, to a T-J and turn R to the rd (797/170), and cross this, onto the BW opposite.

❹ Go past the horse jumps, then R through a rusty gate, and keep SA to a rd (787/155). Go SA, over the rd, then immediately keep L/SA at the fork, on a DT for 1.85km (1.15m) to a T-J (780/139) just after going under the elec. cables. Turn R, off the DT, and keep/bear L, DH to a rd and turn R on this to a X-rds (772/136) into West Marden.

❺ Go SA on the rd for 0.3km (0.2m) then SA on a BW as rd bears sharp L, 0.3km (0.2m) UH to a T-J (766/135). Turn R on the track and shortly R at fork (by houses), to a T-J and go L, for 1km (0.6m) to the wood (756/142). Turn R on a BW (FP only SA), then immediately R at a fork, DH through the woods, to a rd and go R on this, for 0.25km (0.15m) then L on track (Cowdown farm) (768/156).

❻ Keep SA, becoming nice track between the trees, for 3km (1.9m), to a 3-way rd junction (739/155), and go SA or see extension 2. Over a railway bridge, bearing R, then keep L, UH, into Chalton and bear R at the fork (Clanfield / A3) by the Red Lion pub. After 1.1km (0.7m), turn R on a BW (721/166), and keep SA on this, past Gravel hill car park, back to the visitor centre (718/185).

SHORTCUT:

-9.2KM (5.7M) -125 metres of climbing

❶ Turn R at the X-tracks for 0.65km (0.4m) past Foxcombe farm, to a fork and bear L, along the LHS of the woods, for 1.1km (0.7m) to a X-tracks (769/174). Keep SA on this SA/L for 1.4km (0.85m), past Hucksholt farm to a rd.

② Go SA/R on this rd for 0.3km (0.2m) then turn R on a track (770/157) opposite a school, (769/157), past Cowdown farm and rejoin the main route at no.6.

EXTENSION 1:

+10KM (6.3M) 400 metres of climbing

❶ Keep SA on the feint grassy (SDW) track, for 1.2km (0.75m), DH, to the bottom of Beacon Hill, and keep SA, to and over the top. DH, to the X-tracks at the bottom (809/183), and turn L, going steeply DH in the woods.

❷ After 0.65km (0.4m), at the edge of the woods, turn L on a DT, and keep SA on it for 0.5km (0.3m) to a rd (816 /190) and turn R on it. 0.8km (0.5m) to a T-J and go R, into Treyford, over a stream and go R on a (dead end) rd (824/184). Steep UH, for 1km (0.65m) levels out, and turn L on a BW coming across the DT (821/179), on SDW.

❸ After 0.55km (0.35m), bear R at a feint fork (easy to miss) on a BW (820/174) (leaving the SDW, DT), into the woods. DH, for 0.4m and bear R on a DT past the houses, joining a rd. Follow this for 0.25km (0.15m) past the Royal Oak pub, then R on a R.O.W. (814/160).

❹ After 0.9km (0.55m) bear L at a fork, on a BW, down a drive, to another DT (811/169) and turn R on this. After 0.8km (0.5m), past a posh house, to a fork and bear L. After 0.65km (0.4m) on this, turn L on a grassy BW (shortly after going through a gate) (805/179).

❺ Go DH to a T-J at the bottom (by a wooden circular fence) and turn L and follow this BW, bearing R to a rd (797/170) and go SA on a BW, rejoining the main route at no.4.

EXTENSION 2:

+5.8KM (3.6M) 180 metres of climbing

Ⓐ Turn R on the rd for 0.55km (0.35m) to Woodcroft farm and bear R on the Sussex Border Path. After 2km (1.25m), UH, bear L on the DT, (755/169) leaving the SBP (FP only, SA), for 0.55km (0.35m), then keep SA/L on the BW, leaving the DT as it bears R, steep UH.

Ⓑ 0.8km (0.5m) to a T-J by Ditcham school and turn R on this for 0.4km (0.25m) then L on a BW (750/182) into the woods. After 0.25km (0.15m) bear R, for 0.3km (0.2m) then keep SA on the BW as the DT bears L, for 0.9km (0.55m) to a DT (SDW) (748/194) (been here before).

Ⓒ Turn L and retrace your earlier tracks i.e. keep SA for 1.6km (1m) and go SA through the car park (733/198), bearing L, UH, to where you left the Orange trail (729/192) on the R. Follow the rest of the orange route, SA/L inside the woods back to the visitor centre (719/185).

GETTING THERE: The ride starts from the Queens Elizabeth Country park car park which is just south of Petersfield (nr Clanfield), off the A3. Follow the brown signs for the QECP, to the visitors centre and car park (718/185) which costs £1 or £1.50 on Sunday, for the whole day. Train station in Petersfield - go south on the B2070 and join the route by Buriton/no.2.

ACCOMMODATION: B&B at Heath Farmhouse on: 01730 264709, B&B in Petersfield on: 01730 268829. Petersfield T.I. on: 01730 268829

BIKE SHOPS: The Sensible Bicycle Co. on: 01730 266 554 and Owens Cycles on: 01730 260446, both in Petersfield.

REFRESHMENTS: There is a café at the at the start/end, at the visitors centre. there are pubs on the route in West Marden, Charlton, and also in Hooksway on extension 1.

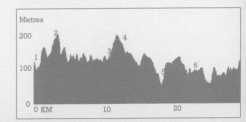

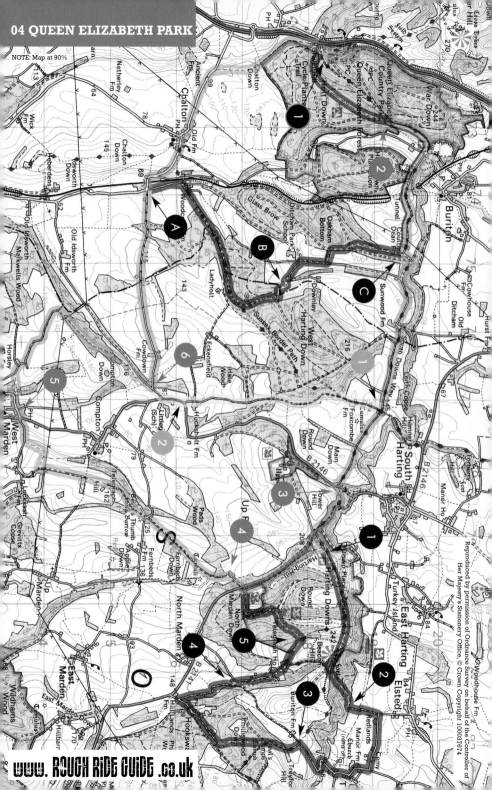

04 QUEEN ELIZABETH PARK

NOTE: Map at 90%

www.ROUGH RIDE GUIDE.co.uk

28.2KM (17.5M) 745 metres of climbing

❶ START. From the visitor centre, go to the Woodland area sign (SU 719/185), and turn R, following the orange wooden posts. After 0.4km (0.25m) turn L, UH on a DT, just before a rd and Gravel hill car park just ahead. To a minor rd then turn L on this, then L again at the 2nd orange post, into the woods. Follow the orange markers (parallel to the A3 rd), bearing sharp R, then L, DH across a track, and keep SA, UH to a T-J with a DT (792/192).

❷ Turn L on this DT (South Downs Way) leaving the cycle trail, and keep SA on this DT, bearing R and DH. Go through the car park to the 3-way rd junction (733/198), and go SA on the rd (SDW). Keep SA for 2.8km (1.75m) (changing surfaces) then bear R off the rd, between some buildings, just after a sharp LH bend by Sundown farm (759/193). Follow the SDW for 1.3km (0.8m) to a X-tracks (771/191) and keep SA or see the shortcut.

❸ 1.3km (0.8m) to the B2146 rd, and go SA on the SDW, parallel to rd, for 0.8km (0.5m) then bear L, over the rd (789/181). After 0.25km (0.15m) on Harting Downs, turn R on the BW (791/182) or see extension 1. Follow this BW for 1.4km (0.85m), parallel to the rd, to a T-J and turn R to the rd (797/170), and cross this, onto the BW opposite.

❹ Go past the horse jumps, then R through a rusty gate, and keep SA to a rd (787/155). Go SA, over the rd, then immediately keep L/SA at the fork, on a DT for 1.85km (1.15m) to a T-J (780/139) just after going under the elec. cables. Turn R, off the DT, and keep/bear L, DH to a rd and turn R on this to a X-rds (772/136) into West Marden.

❺ Go SA on the rd for 0.3km (0.2m) then SA on a BW as rd bears sharp L, 0.3km (0.2m) UH to a T-J (766/135). Turn R on the track and shortly R at fork (by houses), to a T-J and go L, for 1km (0.6m) to the wood (756/142). Turn R on a BW (FP only SA), then immediately R at a fork, DH through the woods, to a rd and go R on this, for 0.25km (0.15m) then L on track (Cowdown farm) (768/156).

❻ Keep SA, becoming nice track between the trees, for 3km (1.9m), to a 3-way rd junction (739/155), and go SA or see extension 2. Over a railway bridge, bearing R, then keep L, UH, into Chalton and keep R at the fork (Clanfield / A3) by the Red Lion pub. After 1.1km (0.7m), turn R on a BW (721/166), and keep SA on this, past Gravel hill car park, back to the visitor centre (718/185).

SHORTCUT:

-9.2KM (5.7M) -125 metres of climbing

❶ Turn R at the X-tracks for 0.65km (0.4m) past Foxcombe farm, to a fork and bear L, along the LHS of the woods, for 1.1km (0.7m) to a X-tracks (769/174). Keep SA on this SA/L for 1.4km (0.85m), past Hucksholt farm to a rd.

❷ Go SA/R on this rd for 0.3km (0.2m) then turn R on a track (770/157) opposite a school, (769/157), past Cowdown farm and rejoin the main route at no.6.

EXTENSION 1:

+10KM (6.3M) 400 metres of climbing

❶ Keep SA on the feint grassy (SDW) track, for 1.2km (0.75m), DH, to the bottom of Beacon Hill, and keep SA, to and over the top. DH, to the X-tracks at the bottom (809/183), and turn L, going steeply DH in the woods.

❷ After 0.65km (0.4m), at the edge of the woods, turn L on a DT, and keep SA on it for 0.5km (0.3m) to a rd (816 /190) and turn R on it. 0.8km (0.5m) to a T-J and go R, into Treyford, over a stream and go R on a (dead end) rd (824/184). Steep UH, for 1km (0.65m) levels out, and turn L on a BW coming across the DT (821/179), on SDW.

❸ After 0.55km (0.35m), bear R at a feint fork (easy to miss) on a BW (820/174) (leaving the SDW, DT), into the woods. DH, for 0.4km and bear R on a DT past the houses, joining a rd. Follow this for 0.25km (0.15m) past the Royal Oak pub, then R on a R.O.W. (814/160).

❹ After 0.9km (0.55m) bear L at a fork, on a BW, down a drive, to another DT (811/169) and turn R on this. After 0.8km (0.5m), past a posh house, to a fork and bear L. After 0.65km (0.4m), turn L on a grassy BW (shortly after going through a gate) (805/179).

❺ Go DH to a T-J at the bottom (by a wooden circular fence) and turn L and follow this BW, bearing R to a rd (797/170) and go SA on a BW, rejoining the main route at no.4.

EXTENSION 2:

+5.8KM (3.6M) 180 metres of climbing

Ⓐ Turn R on the rd for 0.55km (0.35m) to Woodcroft farm and bear R on the Sussex Border Path. After 2km (1.25m), UH, and bear L on the DT, (755/169) leaving the SBP (FP only, SA), for 0.55km (0.35m), then keep SA/L on the BW, leaving the DT as it bears R, steep UH.

Ⓑ 0.8km (0.5m) to a T-J by Ditcham school and turn R on this for 0.4km (0.25m) then L on a BW (750/182) into the woods. After 0.25km (0.15m) bear R, for 0.3km (0.2m) then keep SA on the BW as the DT bears L, for 0.9km (0.55m) to a DT (SDW) (748/194) (been here before).

Ⓒ Turn L and retrace your earlier tracks i.e. keep SA for 1.6km (1m) and go SA through the car park (733/198), bearing L, UH, to where you left the Orange trail (729/192) on the R. Follow the rest of the orange route, SA/L inside the woods back to the visitor centre (719/185).

GETTING THERE: The ride starts from the Queens Elizabeth Country park car park which is just south of Petersfield (nr Clanfield), off the A3. Follow the brown signs for the QECP, to the visitors centre and car park (718/185) which costs £1 or £1.50 on Sunday, for the whole day. Train station in Petersfield - go south on the B2070 and join the route by Buriton/no.2.

ACCOMMODATION: B&B at Heath Farmhouse on: 01730 264709, B&B in Petersfield on: 01730 268829. Petersfield T.I. on: 01730 268829

BIKE SHOPS: The Sensible Bicycle Co. on: 01730 266 554 and Owens Cycles on: 01730 260446, both in Petersfield.

REFRESHMENTS: There is a café at the at the start/end, at the visitors centre. there are pubs on the route in West Marden, Charlton, and also in Hooksway on extension 1.

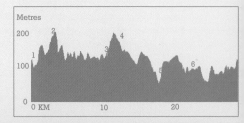

NOTE: Map at 80%

42.8KM (26.6M) 935 metres of climbing

1 START. Go north across the grass, to a BW, and turn L on this, for 0.8km (0.5m), to a X-tracks (SU887/364), and turn L on a BW, or see extension. Go past a car park, joining a drive, to the A287 rd (885/362) and turn R on this rd. After 1.6km (1m), turn L on a ByW (870/364), after the shops, DH, for 0.8km (0.5m) to a rd (866/358). Turn R on this for 0.25km (0.15m) to a fork and bear L (Whitmoor vale), UH, for 0.25km (0.15m) then turn L on a ByW (861/359). 0.5km (0.3m), UH, along the edge of the woods, to a rd, and turn L on this to a T-J with the B3002. Turn R on this for 0.1km then turn L on a BW to Ludshott common, for 0.3km (0.2m) to a X-tracks (854/355).

2 Turn L, for 0.3km (0.2m) then turn R (857/353) on a BW. Keep SA on this for 1.3km (0.8m) (SA at some X-tracks, for another 0.15km), to a fork (847/349). Bear R (847/346). 0.7km (0.45m) to another fork and bear L, which becomes a ByW, for 0.9km (0.55m) to a rd (833/347). Turn L on this (Gentles lane) rd, for 0.65km (0.4m), DH, to a T-J (829/342), and turn R. Keep L, through Passfield on Passfield rd, to the B3004 rd, and go SA on a track, then immediately L on a BW (820/336). Through some woods, joining a rd in Conford, for 0.1km then turn R on a BW (823/330), back into the woods.

3 Over a footbridge, UH, on the (main track) BW, for 0.9km (0.55m) to a bridge over the A3 (821/322).Into the wood, for 0.9km, by a gate. Turn L on the rd for 0.15km then turn R on a ByW (824/318) (Campsite & hotel), to a 3-way junction. Take the central BW, UH, bearing L into the woods, and keep SA over some X-tracks, joining a track. Keep SA at the end of the track, on the BW, to a fork (818/304), and bear R. Keep SA on this for 1km (0.65m) along the edge of the woods, to a X-tracks (812/297), and turn sharp L on the Sussex Border Path (SBP).

4 Follow the SBP, bearing R at the tarmac after 0.15m, past a lake on the LHS, for 0.8km (0.5m) to a fork (just past Home park estate on the RHS). Bear L, leaving the SBP which goes R), on a ST BW, which joins a rd, and bears R, over the railway, to the B2020 rd. Cross the rd and turn R on a BW, along the golf course, to a X-tracks (832/292). Turn L, on the SBP for 1.95km (1.2m) to a 3-way rd junction, and go SA then immediately R (847/305)on the SBP. 1.3km (0.8m) to some X-tracks (858/306) and turn L on a BW (the SBP, SA is a FP). 0.65km (0.4m) to a house (857/312), and turn R, back on the Sussex Border Path.

5 Keep SA on the (grassy) SBP at a X-tracks R into the woods, for 0.15km then L following the fence to a rd (866/313). Turn R on the rd for 0.3km (0.2m) then turn L on Linchmere rd, then immediately R at a fork, on the SBP (868/311). After 1.2km (0.75m), join a drive, bear L at the fork (880/312), (leaving the SBP), on a BW, to a rd (884/313). Go SA on a BW, into the woods, for 0.9km (0.55m) (rejoins the SBP) to a fork (892/314) and turn R on a ST BW, leaving the SBP. Along the hill, then DH to the A286 rd, and turn R on this, UH, for 0.55km (0.35m), then turn L on a BW, (895/305) on Hatch lane.

6 Keep SA/L on the BW, for 0.8km (0.5m) to a T-J (with a FP) and turn L on the BW. 0.4km (0.25m), to the side of a house, on a T-J, and turn L. UH, on this ByW for 0.25km (0.15m), to a (track) T-J (906/300). Turn R and follow the BW for 1.3km (0.8m) to a fork and bear R, joining a track and bearing L on this, to a rd (914/289). NOTE: There are a lot more trails in Black Down, than the map shows. Go SA (on the LHS) BW, going steeply UH, to a view point (919/292). Head north, along the ridge, joining the SBP after 1.2km (0.75m) and turn R on this, and follow it, past a couple of car parks, and bearing R, steeply DH on a ST, to a rd (927/304).

7 Turn L on the rd for 0.5km (0.3m) to a fork and bear R, DH, on Jays lane, for 0.4km (0.25m) then turn L on a BW (931/311). Follow this BW for 1km (0.65m) through woods and a stream, joining a track and keep SA, to a rd (933/321). Go SA on the BW opposite, UH, along the field edge, to a tarmac track and turn L on this, to a rd. Turn R on the rd for 0.25km (0.15m) then turn L on a BW (drive) (933/329), and keep SA on the BW, by a big house (Furnace place). After 0.55km (0.35m) past some ponds, to a junction and keep SA, through farm, UH, to top, then DH, to a rd (918/337).

8 Turn R on the rd, for 0.55km (0.35m) to a fork and bear L (Grayswood), for 0.5km (0.3m) to the A286 rd. Turn R on this for 0.15km (0.1m) then L on a BW (917/348), after the church. UH, for 0.5km (0.3m) (under a railway bridge) to a T-J (914/350) and turn L on the BW, UH, for 1km (0.6m) to a T-J in the woods (907/351). Turn R on the BW (forest track), and keep SA on this BW, UH, bearing L at a (BW) fork, to a X-tracks (900/358) with a ByW. Turn L, UH, to a X-tracks with the Greensands way, and go SA on the ByW. Keep SA on this ByW, for 0.8km (0.5m) parallel with, then to the A3 rd, and (carefully) cross this rd, back to the car park (890/357).

EXTENSION:

+7.9KM (4.9M) 225 metres of climbing

1 Go SA on a good BW track, (not R on the BW going steeply DH), for 0.5km (0.3m) to a fork (by a memorial) and bear L, leaving the DT (887/369). DH, for 0.8km (0.5m) and bear L at the fork (easy to miss), DH, on a ST, for 0.8km (0.5m) to a rd at the bottom (886/ 384). Turn R on the rd, for 0.3km (0.2m) then keep SA on a ByW, as the rd bears sharp L. Past a farm, onto a dark track, DH, over the footbridge at the bottom, and bear R, UH, on the ByW.

2 Turn L at the tarmac drive, to a grass triangle (896/384) and turn R on the Greensands way (GSW) ByW. Follow this, for 1.8km (1.1m) to the A3 rd (896/368) and go SA on the (GSW) ByW. Follow this ByW track for another 2km (1.25m) (bearing R after 1.1km/0.7m, leaving the GSW (989/358)), parallel, to the A3 rd. Cross the A3 rd (carefully), back to the cafe and car park (890/357) and rejoin the main route.

GETTING THERE: This ride starts from the in Devil's Punch Bowl (National Trust) car park on Hindhead common (890/357). This is just off the A3, north of Haslemere, by the Devil's bowl cafe. There is a train station in Haslemere and Liphook.

ACCOMMODATION: B&B's in Haslemere on: 01428 653120 and 658023. YHA at the Devils punchbowl on: 0870 7705864. Camping at Deers Hut pub Liphook 01428 724406. Haslemere Tourist info on: 645425.

BIKE SHOPS: Nothing in Haslemere. Liphook Cycles in Liphook: 01428 727858 and Cycleworks in Guildford: 01483 300380.

REFRESHMENTS: A National trust cafe at the start / end of the ride, and pubs in Conford, Griggs Green, Wheatsheaf common, Grayswood and lots of choice in Haslemere.

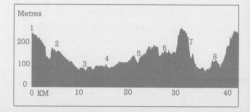

06 PUTTENHAM COMMON

NOTE: Map at 90%

www.ROUGH RIDE GUIDE.co.uk

Reproduced by permission of Ordnance Survey on behalf of the Controller
of Her Majesty's Stationery Office, © Crown Copyright 100037674

21.5KM (13.4M) 375 metres climbing

1 Join the Greensand Way (GSW) BW, on the northern edge of the car park, heading east. After 0.55km (0.35m) keep SA/L (leaving the GSW), shortly to a fork (SU 882/429) and keep L on the BW. Go past Hakley farm, to a X-tracks (895/435) and turn L (Westbrook hill rd).

2 0.9km (0.55m) to a triangle, in Elstead (904/434) and turn L (Thursley rd) for 0.3km (0.2m) to a large triangle (906/436). Turn L on the B3001 for 1km (0.65m) then R on Seale rd (898/440), for 0.65km (0.4m) then turn R on a BW (898/446).

3 0.8km (0.5m) to a rd, past Fullbrook farm, and keep SA on the BW, for 0.8km (0.5m) to a rd. Turn L on this rd for 0.1km then turn R on a BW (913/450), through the woods to Cutt mill ponds. Follow this BW around the ponds and house, UH, to a minor rd (919/456).

4 Keep SA/R on this rd, past Rodsall manor, to a T-J (921/462) and turn L on this rd. After 0.15km (0.1m), turn R (920/460), and keep SA (north), through a car park, on the BW for 0.85m, to a T-J, with the North downs way (917/473). Turn L on the NDW for 0.65km (0.4m), then turn L on a BW (911/473), just before a stream.

5 0.4km (0.25m) to a X-tracks and go R, to the top, and keep R on the LHS of the ponds for 1.5km (0.95m), through a car park, to a rd (912/458). Turn R, to a X-rds, and go SA, for 1km (0.6m) then R on a BW (you cam along earlier), by Fullbrook farm (906/446), for 0.8km (0.5m) to a rd and go SA on the BW.

6 Keep SA/R on the BW, into the woods, for 0.55km (0.35m) to a minor rd/BW (893/444) and turn R on this. 0.7km (0.45m) to a X-tracks, and keep SA on the BW, for 0.9km (0.55m) through the woods, to a (BW) fork (885/458 and bear L. 0.5km (0.3m) to a rd (881/459), by a transmitter, and turn L.

7 After 0.25km (0.15m) keep SA on a ByW, as the rd ends / bears R, for 0.15km (0.1m) to a fork and bear R on a BW, to a rd and go L on this for 0.1km then R on a BW/drive (878/455). 0.4km (0.25m) to the B3001 rd and turn R on this, for 0.25km (0.15m) then turn L on the (GSW) ByW (872/454).

8 Follow this (R at a fork) for 0.9km (0.55m) to a rd, and go SA on the GSW, for 0.4km (0.25m) to a T-J. Turn L, for 0.3km (0.2m) (joining a drive, then leaving it), and bear R, on the GSW (872/439). Alongside the river, to a rd (874/434).

9 Turn R, over a bridge and bear L at the triangle, to a T-J, and turn L on Tilgate rd, for 0.3km (0.2m) back to the car park, on the L (874/429).

EXTENSION OPTIONS:

Various

There are some good commons around this area, that are worth exploring further, and will enable you to ride as little or as much as you like.

1 **Puttenham Common** - This is on the route, and perfect to explore a bit further.

2 **Frensham Common** - Has 2 easy cycle loops, one is 1.5km or both loops together are 5.5km. See www.waverley.gov.uk/countryside/frenshamcycletrail.asp

3 **Hankley Common** - This is an army training ground, with some nice bridleway tracks. The sandy terrain drains well, but deep patches can be a pain, especially when dry.

4 **Witley Common** - Some good single track. The area south of the A3 is a Nature Reserve though.

•NOTE: This is a sandy area, so although the trails drain quite well, where there are deep patches of sand, it can be difficult to cycle.

GETTING THERE: Where you start this ride will depend where you are coming from. Puttenham is easy just off the A31, Elstead off the A3, or from the car park (on Tilford road) in Tilford, where we started from (875/429). Train station in Farnham, 4km/2.5m away - from the station, head SE on Tilford road (off Waverley lane/B3001) to Tilford.

ACCOMMODATION: B&B at South Lodge (nr Alice holt forest), on: 01420 520960, B&B in Tilford on: 01252 792009. YHA in Hindhead on: 0870 7705864, Camping nr Churt on: 01428 712090, Farnham T.I. on: 01252 715109.

BIKE SHOPS: East St Cycles in Farnham on 01252 723888 (around GR 841/470).

REFRESHMENTS: There are pubs in Tilford, Elstead, and Charleshill.

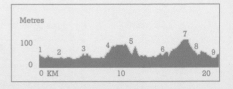

CHICHESTER DISTRICT

28KM (17.4M) 705 metres of climbing

1 START. At the post office (by the Blue Bell pub) (SU 878/176), turn onto Mill lane, then bear R immediately, behind the back of the PO. After 0.25km, past the church, and keep SA/L on a BW, as the rd bears L, and follow this SA, UH, for 0.8km (0.5m) to a T-J by Hill farm (878/166).

2 Turn L, for a tough UH on the (SDW) DT, for 3.4km (2.1m) (or see the Short Ride), then turn R on a BW, off the SDW (910/164) (before the this track starts going DH). After 0.5m keep R/SA at a fork, then shortly keep L/SA on a BW, leaving the DT which bears R (907/154).

3 Exit the woods through a wooden gate, through some more gates, DH, to a DT and turn L to a rd. Turn R on the rd, DH to a T-J (906/131) (by Droke farm) and turn R. 0.3km to a fork and bear L on Eastdean hill (Goodwood).

4 After 1.45km (0.9m) turn R on a BW just before a T-J (904/116), running parallel then rejoining the rd after 0.9km (0.55m). Keep SA/R on the rd for 1.6km (1m) (alongside the Goodwood horse race track) to a T-J (882/107) and turn R on the rd, UH.

5 After 0.25km (0.15m) turn L through car park no.6 on a BW (881/110) bearing L and UH. To the (Seven points) car park (871/110) and go SA on a gravel track, shortly to a fork and bear L on a BW, DH, through the fields.

6 1.6km (1m), fast grassy ST, steep DH, to a X-tracks (by a gate at bottom of the field) (856/107). Go SA, over a brick bridge, then a wooden bridge, and keep SA to a rd.

7 Turn R on the cycleway on the RHS of the rd for 50 meters then turn L over the rd onto Binderton lane (850/108). After 0.4km (0.25m) keep SA, as the rd bears L, onto a DT and keep SA on this to the rd (834/117). Turn R on this for 1.1km (0.7m) (or see the extension) then turn R on a rd (Brickkiln farm) (835/128).

8 Follow this rd for 1.1km (0.7m) to a X-rds and keep SA for another 1.1km (0.7m) to a T-J (846/146) (BW, SA). Turn L on the rd for 0.7km (0.45m) (843/152) then keep SA as the rd bears sharp L, dropping down onto a BW, and turn R on this.

9 Keep SA on this main DT to a T-J with the SDW (849/171) by a water tank. Go SA over the DT, bearing R through a field (feint track) down to the trees and through a small entrance into the woods (852/172).

10 DH, to a DT (859/176) and turn R, UH for 0.55km (0.35m) to a T-J (862/174). Turn L out of the woods, DH for 1km (0.65m) to a T-J (871/171) and turn L. 0.65km (0.4m) to a rd (873/177) and turn R, under a bridge, back into Cocking by the Blue Bell pub and PO (878/176).

SHORT RIDE:

12KM (7.5M) 365 metres of climbing

Follow the start of the main route until instructed otherwise.

1 After 1.6km (1m) turn R on a BW (X-tracks) (894/165) and turn R, and follow this BW, SA, DH. Exit the wood after 1.65km (1m) at Burntoak Gate and keep SA on a better (BW) track to a X-tracks (889/145). Turn L on the BW, which bears sharp L to a T-J (890/141) and turn L, and follow this BW into the woods.

2 Shortly at a fork (900/149) keep L, on the BW, UH, and follow this DT/BW for 1.6km (1m), all the way to the top (904/165), to a X-tracks with the SDW. Go SA on the BW opposite, for a fast and fun DH, keeping L at a fork with a good track, for 0.65km (0.4m) to a rd (892/175) and keep SA/L on this, for 1.6km (1m), back into Cocking (878/176).

EXTENSION:

+13.6KM (8.5M) +400 metres climbing

1 Turn R on the rd, then shortly L on a BW (833/119) steep UH for 1km, to a X-tracks (828/124) and turn L, then shortly L again at another X-tracks. Follow this BW, climbing gradually for 1.3km (0.8m) to a X-tracks (825/112) and keep SA, past a trip point on the BW for 1.6km (1m), across the top/open, back into the trees, then out to a X-tracks (813/105).

2 Turn L then shortly R at a T-J, and follow this BW, keeping L at a fork (809/103), great DH for over 2km's (1.25m) to a drive (796/089) and turn R towards Adsden House. Keep L on this track for 2km (1.25m), UH, then shortly after you start going DH turn R off this track, onto a BW (793/105) (Walderton Down).

3 Follow this BW, turning R, then L by building (800/103), and keep SA to the X-tracks you were at earlier (813/105). Turn L, then shortly R on a BW, into the woods (811/106) and follow this BW across the top of the hill again (but on LHS) for 1.6km (1m) then keep SA on the BW, leaving the main track.

4 Shortly turn L at T-J, for 0.6km (0.4m), joining a DT, to a X-tracks (824/121) and turn R on the Monarchs Way and keep SA, following this back (steep) DH, bearing R on another track, DH, to a rd (835/128) and go SA on the rd opposite, by Brickkiln farm) to rejoin the route at no.8.

GETTING THERE: The ride starts in Cocking village, on the A286, south of Midhurst (where the A272 crosses the A286). Parking is limited within the village, but there is a car park just outside the village, south on the A286, at the top of the hill, on the right (by the Bepton organics sign). Railway station in Chichester (8km/5m) follow the (Sustrans) Centurion Way cyclepath, north to West Dean.

ACCOMMODATION: B&B at 'The Fox goes free' in Charlton on: 01243 811461, B&B at 'Lodge Hill Farm' in West Dean on: 01243 535245, Camping & caravanning near Graffham on: 01798 867476 or Goodwood on: 01243 755 033/022. Chichester TI: 01243 775888.

BIKE SHOPS: Midhurst sports shop has a few basic bike bits, otherwise try The Sensible Bicycle Co. in Petersfield (on the A3) on: 01730 266 554.

REFRESHMENTS: A pub and post office shop in Cocking at the start / end of the ride and a pub in East Dean. Also a pub in Chilgrove on extension 1, and a pub in Charlton on the shortcut.

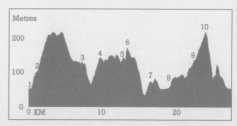

09 ARUNDEL

24.5KM (15.2M) 515 metres of climbing

1 START. Follow Mill rd off the High street (just north of the river) (TQ 019/070), heading north, for 2.25km (1.4m) past Swanbourne Lake, to a junction in Offham. Turn L, then immediately R on a BW beside a house, (025/088), DH, and go SA, across a field, keeping close to a wood on your LHS.

2 Up to and through a gate, and go L, onto a farm track, to South Stoke farm (025/099). Stay on the BW, around field edge, then dropping down, and along the river for 2.75km (1.7m), then L, UH, on South Lane, to the B2139 rd (018/115).

3 Turn L on the rd, then just past the pub bear R on a BW, staying on LHS of hedge, UH, keeping SA at a drive, into the woods, then across a field, through a gate, to a rd (002/110). Go SA on the BW, into Houghton Forest, and join a DT, keeping R on this, or L to the car park and snack hut.

4 DH, following the blue BW signs, then green cycleway signs, keeping SA/L leaving the DT, out of the woods, to a grassy T-J (SU 988/113). Keep R, UH, to a X-tracks at the top, and keep SA, on the Monarchs way for 0.45km (0.25m) then turn L on a BW (969/126).

5 Superb long DH, through Great Bottom, keeping SA, DH on this BW for 3.55km (2.2m) to a X-tracks, and keep L, DH, into the woods, for another 0.85km (0.55m) to a rd (969/ 085). Go SA (R then L) at the triangle, on the BW opposite, follow this DT for 0.95km (0.55m) then turn L on a BW, just past a forest DT (978/080).

6 UH for 1km (06m) to junction with a DT (984/087) and turn R on the DT for 0.75km (0.45m) to a X-tracks (991/ 084). See note. Turn L on the DT, UH, and keep turning R, heading south east, along the edge of Screens Wood.

• **NOTE:** We are not sure of the access rights to this next section, as there is nothing official, but people use it with no problems. If in doubt and fear that any conflict may ensue, please use the BW SA.

7 Keep SA, DH, on this fun track, over a DT, following the BW, to the A27 rd (TQ 012/069). Turn L to the round-about and take the 2nd exit, on Maltravers St, into Arundel, back to the High St (018/071) and turn R, back to the car park.

TOP TIP: Houghton Forest has some nice trails worth exploring, whether you want to extend your ride, or just have a short ride around these woods. There is also a snack hut, so it makes a good place for the more energetic riders to go off exploring while others have a breather.

There are lots of great woodland tracks on this ride.

GETTING THERE: The ride starts from Arudel, which is on the A27. There are car parks in Arundel on Queens rd, Mill rd and Rivers rd. There is also a car park at Houghton Forest, on the route (001/108). Train station in Arundel and also in Amberley.

ACCOMMODATION: B&B at Arundel house on: 01903 882136, B&B in Charlton in 'The Fox goes free' on: 01243 811461. YHA in Arundel on: 0870 7705676 Camping at Gumber Bothy farm (GR 961/118), tel: 01243 814484 but has no road access, Chichester T.I. on: 01243 775888 and Arundel T.I. on: 01903 882268.

BIKE SHOPS: South Downs Bikes in Storrington on 01903 745534/743208 and also in Angmering (nr Littlehampton) on 01903 770649.

REFRESHMENTS: Various in Arundel, a pub in Offam, and another in Houghton, a snack hut in the Houghton Forest car park, and a couple of pubs in Slindon (just off the route).

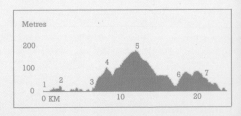

39.4KM (24.5M) 1,000 metres climbing

1 **START**. Go along Westcott St to a fork (TQ137/489) and bear L (Balchins lane) for 0.5km (0.3m) then R a BW (134/486). Keep SA for 0.65km (0.4m) to a fork (128/485) and bear R, for 0.8km (0.5m) to a DT by farm (121/483). Bear L then R (SA) between the barns, alongside the woods, for 1km (0.6m) to a rd (112/482) and go R.

2 UH, for 1.1km (0.7m) then turn L off the rd onto a ST (known as Blind terror) (115/492) near a FP and BW on the R. 0.5km (0.3m) parallel to the rd, to a DT and turn L on this (ByW) (113/497). 0.4km (0.25m) to a fork and bear L, on a DT ByW and keep SA. 1.1km (0.7m), SA at the X-tracks, to a fork (100/491) and bear R, on the NDW.

3 Follow this main DT for 2.7km (1.65m) to a T-J (077/489), and turn R for 0.1km (1m) L at a 3-way split. After 0.55km (0.35m), just past a farm, turn L on a BW as the rd bears sharp R (072/489). DH, under the A25 to a rd, in Shere, and go SA (Middle street) for 0.3km (0.2m), then turn R (Pathfields cul-d-sac) (072/476).

4 Keep SA on the BW, into the woods and bear L, then R at the first a fork, then very shortly L at another fork, to a rd. Go SA on the BW, to a T-J and turn L to a railway crossing (069/467), and cross this (carefully). Turn R on the ByW, for 1.95km (1.2m), becoming a rd, and keep SA over a log, on a BW, when rd bears sharp R (065/449).

5 0.25km (0.15m) to a rd and turn L on this, then R at a (just before the houses), on a BW, into the woods. Follow the BW signs for 2.2km (1.35m) to a T-J with another BW, and turn L, UH, to a rd (067/426). Turn R on the rd, then immediately L, on a BW. 0.9km (0.55m) DH then L on a BW (just past a house) (067/418), to a drive and go R.

6 Follow the drive to a rd (073/418), and turn L on this, for 0.4km (0.25m), then turn R on a BW (074/ 422), for 0.65km (0.4m) to a rd (080/424). Turn R on this rd (or a Quarry on L, for playing in), for 0.5km (0.3m) past the Windmill pub, and bear L off the main rd, for 0.15km (0.1m) then turn L on a (Private drive) BW, UH then DH (084/421).

7 0.8km (0.5m) to a fork and bear R, for 0.9km (0.55m) to another fork and bear L, for 0.4km (0.25m) to another fork, and bear R. After 0.5km (0.3m), by the cemetery, turn R just after the green barrier, on a rutted BW, DH to Peaslake church and go SA to a rd (086/447) and turn R.

8 Past Hurtwood Inn, to a X-rds, with bus stop & (the very good) Peaslake shop SA. Turn R, then shortly L on Radnor rd (086/447), UH, for 2km (1.25m) or see extension 1.

9 Turn L (098/431) on bumpy track, UH, into a car park, and go SA past the metal barriers, to a fork and bear R. Past some stagnant water, to the top (viewpoint on the R - the BW going steep DH here is known as Widow maker) and turn L on a DT (103/430). After 0.25km (0.15m), turn R on a ST (known as Parklife) (103/431) and follow this to a DT (the end of the ST) (105/435).

10 Turn R on the DT, to a X-tracks, and bear L on a feint ST (Telegraph road) (in between the DT's going SA and L), under the telegraph lines. Keep SA on this over other tracks for 1.2km (0.75m) to a slight clearing and turn R on a ST (known as Mutiny) (104/448), DH to a rd (108/451).

11 Turn R on the rd, for 1.4km (0.85m), then turn L on Pasture wood rd (112/440), for 0.25km (0.15m) and go SA on the Greensand way (GSW) BW, as the rd bears L. After 1.85km (1.15m) go R at the T-J on the GSW, bearing L, to a rd and SA on the BW, UH to Leith tower (139/432).

12 Turn L on the good BW track just before the (snack shop) tower, (steep BW DH on the R is known as Cliff Richard), keeping SA for 0.4km (0.25m), then bear R on a ST (137/434). To a fork and bear L on a ST (known as Caspers; ST on R is known as Trout mask replica) DH, for 1km (0.6m) to a T-J with a FP (136/445) and turn L.

13 0.3km (0.2m) to a X-tracks (133/445), then R on a BW (133/445). Keep SA, DH, on the BW (becoming a drive) for 1.2km (0.75m), then keep SA on a BW (not R, on the DT BW), as the rd turns L by the stables (135/456). To a DT and go SA, past the houses, UH on a ST, to a X-tracks at the top (140/459) and go L or see extension 2.

14 Follow this sandy ByW (or on the better ST on the sides) for 1.6km (1m), then turn R on a BW, by a wooden post (easy to miss) (132/473). To a drive and turn R, to the A25 rd, and turn R on this, back into Westcott and your car (141/485).

EXTENSION 1:
+2.9km (1.8M) & 100 metres climbing

1 1.3km (0.8m) UH on the rd, then R (opposite a worksite entrance) (094/437), to a feint ST fork and bear L (wooden posts on R ST). Follow this twisty ST (known as Golden Birdies) to a rd (087/443) and turn R. Back into Peaslake village and turn R back UH on Radnor road (086/447), UH, for 2km (1.25m), and rejoin the main route at no.9.

EXTENSION 2:
+3.9KM (2.4M) & +75 metres climbing

A Turn R on the DT for 0.5km (0.3m) to a clearing and join the 'Summer lightening' MTB trail here. Follow this circular waymarked trail all the way around back to here, and turn L back to the X-tracks and go SA, rejoining the main route at no. 14.

SHORTCUT:
Various

Rather than suggesting a shortcut to the main route, park at Holmbury hill car park (GR 098/431) and explore the numerous singletracks in here, Leith hill and Pitch Hill.

GETTING THERE: We started from Nivarna Cycles in Westcott, off the A25, but if you are arriving by car we strongly suggest/ask you park in one of the many public car parks available on the route - which ever one is closest to where you are coming from. Railway stations in Dorking or Gomshall (on the route).

ACCOMMODATION: B&B in Lockhurst Hatch farm on: 01483 202689, or Royal Oak on: 01306 730120 or Hurtwood Inn on: 730851, both in Peaslake. YHA in Holmbury St Mary on: 0870 7705868, Camping in Horsley on: 01483 283273. Guilford T.I. on: 01483 444333 or Dorking T.I. on: 01306 879327.

BIKE SHOPS: Nirvana Cycles in Westcott, on 01306 740300, who do guided rides.

REFRESHMENTS: Shop at Westcott, a snack shop at Leith hill tower, (tea) shop at Peaslake village stores (popular with cyclists). There are also pubs at Shere, Pitch hill, and Holmbury St Mary.

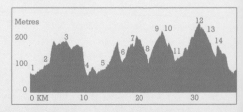

29.6KM (18.4M) 922 metres climbing

❶ START. Head East (on the South Downs Way) steep UH for 1.25km (0.75m) to a T-J (TQ 130/116) and turn R (leaving the SDW), DH for 1.6km (1m) to a X-tracks (121/103). Turn L for 0.5km (0.3m) then bear R through a gate, on a BW (126/101), bearing L, UH, to a rd.

❷ Go SA through a gate into a field, and go SA, UH, to another gate (127/098) and turn L. Past a farm, becoming a ST for 0.5km (0.3m) to a fork and bear L, to a DT, and turn L. At a grass triangle (139/094) turn R on the DT, for 0.65km (0.4m) then go R on the Monarch's Way BW (138/088), DH, to a rd (130/085) and turn L on this, UH.

❸ Turn R at the top (139/085), through a gate to Cissbury ring. Bear R immediately on a BW, by a National Trust sign, then fork L on a BW, around Cissbury Ring. After 1.1km (0.7m) at BW junction (138/074) go L for another 1km (0.6m) to T-J and turn L, through a gate and then R on a BW (142/081), DH. To a gate and bear R, then shortly L through another gate (149/079) and into a field.

❹ 1.5km (0.95m) to (not through) a silver gate at the end (158/068), and turn L through a wooden gate, to a T-J. Turn L onto a grassy ST, to a farm, and bear R on the concrete track (past houses) to a rd (161/ 072), and turn L on this. 0.9km (0.55m) UH, and turn R on a BW (opposite a car park) (162/080) for 0.5km (0.3m) to a fork and bear L.

❺ 0.15km to a X-tracks (elec. pylon on the R) (168/079) and turn L and follow this alongside a fence, and keep SA this ends, to a rd. Keep SA/R on the rd for 0.85km (0.5m) then bear L on the SDW, as the rd bears R, to a DT and bear R/SA to a X-tracks (162/099). Take the BW to the R of the SDW or see the shortcut.

❻ Keep L at T-J, along the egde of the woods, then R, into the woods, DH on this fun ST BW. To a

DT X-tracks (168/117) and turn R (Mouse lane) for 0.55km (0.35m) and bear R on the High street. Bear R on Bramber rd, and SA (at X-rds) on Clays Hill then shortly R on Maudlin rd. After 0.35km (0.2m) on this rd turn R on Sopers lane (180/103).

❼ UH for 2.25km (1.4m), through Maudalin farm, keeping L at a Private rd sign, to a rd at the top (162/094) (been here before). Turn R on the rd for 0.15km and keep SA on the SDW, as the rd bears R, to a DT and bear R/SA back to the X-tracks (162/099).

7A Go SA on the SDW (bearing L) on the SDW, for 2.35km to a X-tracks (144/113).

❽ Turn R on a BW, DH into the woods. Follow it to a car park / X-tracks (145/123) and turn L on the BW, going into the woods. Follow this for 2.2km (1.4m), UH at the end, to a DT (been here before), and turn R, DH, back to the car park (120/120).

SHORTCUT:

-7.3KM (4.5M) 220 meters climbing

❶ Keep SA on the SDW, rejoining the main oute at no.7A.

GETTING THERE: This ride starts just south of Washington, which is off the A24 road, north of Worthing. Turn left on the A283 at a round-about on the A24, and follow the signs for Washington. Go (south) through the village and up the hill to a car park (120/120). Train station in Worthing - head north on the A24 rd for 6.5km (4m), to Findon and the ride.

ACCOMMODATION: B&B in Washington on 01903 893542, and Steyning on: 01903 812286. YHA at Truliegh Hill /Tottington barn (east of Steyning) on: 0870 7706078, Brighton Backpackers on: 01273 777717. Worthing T.I. on: 01903 210022.

BIKE SHOPS : Quest Adventure in Worthing on 01903 573700, or Rayment Cycles on 01273 697617 and Baker Street Bikes 01273 675754 both in Brighton.

REFRESHMENTS: Pub in Washington near the start, pubs and shops in Steyning and off the route (downhill) in Findon.

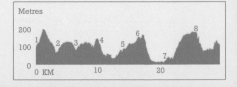

12 DITCHLING MAIN
13 DITCHLING SHORT

NOTE: Map at 95%

Reproduced by permission of Ordnance Survey on behalf of the Controller of Her Majesty's Stationery Office, © Crown Copyright 100037674

www.ROUGH RIDE GUIDE.co.uk

18.7KM (11.6) 495 metres of climbing

1 START. Head **west** away from the rd, through a gate, on BW no.13 (main SDW track) for 0.3km (0.2m), just around a LHB **then turn L** (TQ 330/131) off the main/SDW track, through a gate, **on BW no.16** (Heathy brow). Go DH, for 1.1km (0.7m) to a fork , just past a gate **and bear R on Lower Standean BW** (328/128).

2 DH, into the valley, **through a gate** by the trees, on BW no.37, through a field **and bear R to a** single wooden gate. Immediately **through this turn L** on BW no.38, for 0.1m to a fork **and bear R,** on BW no.39. Keep L on a DT (315/115) **and turn R** on BW no.21.

3 Keep SA at BW no.20, to a gate and turn L on BW no.19, UH, to some X-tracks (309/117). **Turn L,** through a gate onto the West Sussex border path, **and keep SA on** this as the ST gets very feint, **for 2.6km (1.6m)** on the RHS of the field, **through a gate to a rd** (302/095).

4 Turn R, to a T-J (A27 just ahead), **and turn R, keeping SA** at the roundabout for 0.55km (0.35m), bears R, **then turn L** on the (Waterhall) BW (297/096). **Over the A23** and railway, **and turn R, bearing L, UH,** on a DT, to a T-J (291/095) by a barn **and turn R,** UH.

5 1.6km (1m) to a X-tracks (280/107) where the main track bears R, **and go SA** through a silver gate, ST. **After 1km (0.6m)** go through a gate and bear L, DH, through a tunnel of trees **for 0.15km** then R through a gate before the houses and a drive, **and immediately sharp R again,** UH, on a DT (273/115) or see **extension 1.**

6 Keep SA, to a gate by some trees (New Timber hill), **and go SA, DH, on** the grass, to the A23 rd. Go over the bridge (over the A23) **and turn L to a rd** (284/129) **and turn R** on this. Joining the slip rd off the A23, **and keep SA** (Pyecombe/A273) for 0.4km (0.25m) **then turn L on** Church lane (291/124) into Pyecombe.

7 Bear R by the church, on School lane, **to the A273 rd and turn L** on this for 0.25km (0.15m), then turn R over this rd (294/129). On the SDW, through the golf club for 1.1km (0.7m), **through a gate, to a X-tracks** (305/128).

8 Turn L on the SDW, towards the (Jack & Jill) windmills for 0.4km (0.25m) to a T-J (305/132) **and turn R** on the SDW. Keep SA on the main track (SDW) for 3.2km (2m), back to the car park (333/130) or see **extension 2.**

EXTENSION 1:

+5.5KM (3.4M) +185 metres climbing

1 Turn L on the SDW, to a rd (271/114), **then turn R on** the rd, then shortly **L on a BW** parallel to the rd, to a rd in Poynings village (265/120). Turn L on the rd, **then L again** by the church, **through the village,** for 0.3km (0.2m) and turn L on a BW (261/119).

2 Follow this BW, UH, for 1.6km (1m), keeping SA to a rd **and turn L** on this (or R to the pub) for 0.15km (0.1m), **then turn L** on the SDW (258/107). Keep bearing R at the forks in the BW, DH, to a rd at Saddlescombe (270/114). Go over the rd on the SDW, UH, **back to the start of the** extension and rejoin the route at no.6.

EXTENSION 2:

+1.8KM (1.1M) +135 metres climbing

A Turn L at the Keymer post (315/129) (before the Sussex Border Path which is good but can be busy with walkers), DH, (bombholes to the R of main gravel track) **keeping L** at a fork after 0.65km (0.4m), **to a rd** (313/137). Turn R on the rd, for 1.3km (0.8m) **to a X-rds** (325/137) **and turn R on the rd,** steep UH on the infamous climb to Ditchling Beacon (333/130).

B Through a gate after 0.8km (0.5), **to a X-tracks** (369/125), **and keep SA on the SDW.** Keep SA on this for 3.9km (2.4m), past Dews pond, **to a rd and go SA** back to the car park at the end / start (333/130).

SHORT RIDE:

11.2KM (7M) 255 metres of climbing

1 START. Head **East** i.e. cross the rd from the car park, on the (SDW) BW for 0.35m then turn R (post but no BW sign), (338/128). Through some trees, **to a** single gate and bear R on BW no.11, on a feint track through the field, for 1.4m to the farm rd (347/108).

B Bear R/SA on this for 1km (0.65m) to a rd (350/098) and turn L and follow this DT, SA, UH for 3.6km to a X-rds with the SDW at the top (369/125). Turn L, on the SDW, and follow this for 3.75km, all the way back to the start at Ditchling Beacon car park (333/130).

GETTING THERE: Both rides start from the car park at Ditchling Beacon (333/130). This is south of Ditchling village, at the top of the hill, off Ditchling road. There is a railway station at Sussex university, Keymer, and Lewes.

ACCOMODATION: B&B at Poynings Manor farm on: 01273 857371, B&B in Kingston near Lewes on: 01273 472295. YHA in Brighton on: 0870 7705724 Brighton backpackers on: 01273 777717. Brighton T.I. (premium rate) on: 0906 7112255 and Worthing T.I. on: 01903 210022.

BIKE SHOP: Bicycleworks in Lewes on: 01273 483399

REFRESHMENTS: There is often an ice-cream van at the start/end. A pub and tea shop in Pyecombe, and a pub (and maybe an ice cream van) on extension 1, at Devils Dyke.

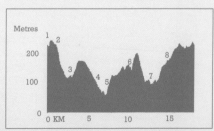

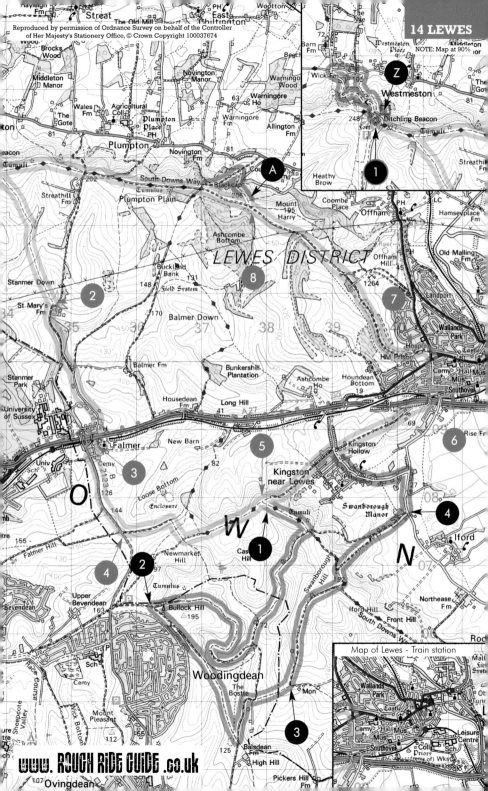

Reproduced by permission of Ordnance Survey on behalf of the Controller
of Her Majesty's Stationery Office, © Crown Copyright 100037674

LEWES DISTRICT

Map of Lewes - Train station

www.RouGH RiDE GUiDE.co.uk

22KM (13.7M) 535 metres of climbing

❶ START. Cross the rd from the car park, going east, on the (SDW) BW for 0.55km (0.35m) then turn R (post but no BW sign), (TQ 338/128). Through some trees, to a single gate and bear R on BW no.11, feint track through the field, for 2.25km (1.4m) to the farm rd (347/108).

❷ Bear R/SA on this for 1.1km (0.7m) to a rd (350/098). Go R/SA on the rd, DH, and keep SA for 1km (0.6m) then bearing R by the A27 rd SA. After 0.1km (0.05m) turn L over the bridge, opposite the Swan inn pub (353/089).

❸ Turn R on the other side of the bridge, then L on Park street, past a pond on the L, bearing R to a T-J with the B2123 rd (352/086). Turn L on the rd, UH, going through a gap in the hedge on the L, parallel to the rd, for a total of 1.3km (0.8m) and turn L on a BW (358/075).

❹ After 1km (0.65m) at a corner of woods, bear R to a gate, through this, and turn immediately R through another gate on the SDW (367/078). UH, to a T-J with a good track (369/074) and go L on this for 0.7m to a fork (379/079) and keep L/SA, leaving the SDW or see extension 1.

❺ DH, on a rutty DT for 1.45km (0.9m), becoming Kingston ridge rd, to a rd in Kingston near Lewes, (390/087) and go SA on the BW. **5A** Follow this for 1.8km (1.1m), over the A27 rd, bearing R, on Juggs rd, and keep SA to the B2193 rd. Turn L on this rd (Southover High st), then immediately L on Bell lane (408/095).

❻ Follow this rd bearing R, becoming Winterbourne Hollow, for 0.65km (0.4m) UH, to a X-rds with the A277 rd. Go SA on Nevill rd for 0.15km (0.1m) then turn L on a BW (405/101) opposite Spital rd.

❼ Keep SA, UH, on this main track (bear to the RHS of a pylon after 3.2km/2m), at the Blackcap hill sign, through a gate) for 3.85km (2.4m) to a fork (377/122) and bear L around the bottom of the hill, or see extension 2.

❽ Through a gate after 0.8km (0.5) to a X-tracks (369/125), and keep SA on the SDW. Keep SA on this for 3.85km (2.4m) past Dews pond, to a rd and go SA back to the start (333/130) or see extension 3.

EXTENSION 1:
+13.7KM (8.5M) 360 metres of climbing

❶ Stay on the SDW for another 0.5m, to a X-tracks (386/075) and turn R. BW, DH, for 1.6km (1m) to a building and keep L, for 0.2m to a X-tracks (377/058) and turn R and follow this BW, UH for 3.1km (1.9m) on Bullock Hill

❷ At the junction past the elec pylon (362/063), turn L, becoming a DH, and keep R at the fork after 1.2km (0.75m) DH for another 1.2km (0.75m), to a X-tracks (375/044). Turn L, down to a juntion and keep SA, off the main track, on a BW, DH, then steep UH.

❸ Turn L on the track at the top (383/052), UH for 1.85km (1.15m) then keep SA on a BW, as the track bears R, to a T-J (391/067). Turn L, on the SDW, then shortly at the X-tracks (390/069), turn R, off the SDW. Steep DH, bearing L, to a T-J, and turn R, down to a rd (401/077).

❹ Turn L on the rd, then first L after 0.55km (0.35m) (401/083), into Kingston near Lewes. After 1.4km (0.85m) just before you leave the village, turn R on a BW (390/087) and rejoin the main route at 5a.

EXTENSION 2:
+0.65KM (0.4M) 60 metres of climbing

Ⓐ Bear R on the BW to the northern side of Blackcap, for fun DH, for 0.55km (0.35m) to a X-tracks (375/128) and turn L, UH, to the top (369/125). Turn R and follow the SDW for 3.7km (2.3m) back to the start (333/130).

EXTENSION 3:
+2.8KM (1.75M) 160 metres of climbing

Ⓩ Turn R on a BW just before the rd (& Ditchling Beacon), fast DH, being careful of walkers and horses. Turn L on the rd at the bottom, for 0.5m (0.3m) to a X-rds (325/138) and turn L, up the infamous Ditchling Beacon hill climb on the rd, back to the car park at the top (333/130).

GETTING THERE: This ride starts from the car park at Ditchling Beacon (333/130). Go south on Ditchling road, from the village of Ditchling village, to the top of the hill, and the car park is on the right (333/130). Railway stations at Sussex university, Keymer, and Lewes.

ACCOMODATION: B&B at Poynings Manor farm on: 01273 857371, B&B in Kingston near Lewes on: 01273 472295. YHA in Brighton on: 0870 7705724 Brighton backpackers on: 01273 777717. Brighton T.I. (premium rate) on: 0906 7112255 and Worthing T.I. on: 01903 210022.

BIKE SHOP: Bicycleworks in Lewes on: 01273 483399.

REFRESHMENTS: There is often an ice-cream van at the start/end. There is a pub in Falmer, Kingston near Lewes, and Lewes.

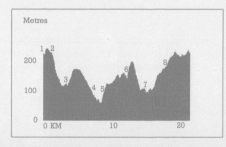

30.6KM (19M) 845 metres of climbing

❶ START. Go through a gate at the north end of the car park, onto a BW and follow this, around the bottom of the wooded hill. After 1km (0.6m), at the houses, turn L then immediately R on a narrow lane, UH. Follow this main track for 2.25km (1.4m), becomes a gravel surface, through a field, back into the woods, to a X-tracks (544/005), by Snap hill.

❷ Turn L (Lullington heath), DH, keeping R at a fork after 0.15km (0.1m) for 0.3km (0.2m) to a multiple (7) junction (541/007). Bear R (Lullington heath), UH, going through a gate into the nature reserve, and follow the BW to a gate and T-J (545/018). Turn L on a (DT) BW, (Litlington) UH for 0.65km (0.4m) to a X-rds, at Winchester's pond.

❸ Keep SA for 0.65km (0.4m) to a fork (532/019) & bear R or see extension 1). 1km (0.65m) DH to a rd (525/025) and turn R on this, and keep SA, UH, for 1km (0.6m) then turn R on the SDW (532/032). Up Wendover hill, for 0.9km (0.55m) to a fork (540/035) and bear R (L is a FP), along the top of a valley, to the summit (544/033).

❹ Keep following the blue SDW signs, along, then down the hill, alongside, then into some woods after 1.95km (1.2m) (553/018). Keep R then SA, DH, steep, technical track, to a (St Andrews) church and keep SA on the rd. To a T-J in Jevington, and turn R then immediately L on Eastbourne Lane (BW), (562/013) or see the shortcut.

❺ UH, rejoining the SDW, for 1.5km (0.95m) to a X-tracks (576/009), and keep SA on the SDW. 2.65km (1.65m) to the A259 rd (585/985). Go SA on the SDW, to a trig point and keep R, to the B2013 rd. Cross the rd, into a car park and turn R for 0.1km, to a gate, and follow the BW (586/979), DH, into the valley.

❻ Keep SA for 3km (1.9m) and bear L, on a drive, just past the farm (563/963), for 0.65km (0.4m) to a rd (564/956). Turn L on the rd, then shortly R, through a gate, on a BW, parallel to the rd (heading west). Later, rejoin the rd, and turn L on this for 0.25km (0.15), then keep SA on the SDW, as the rd bears sharp R.

❼ UH, for 0.3km (0.2m) then bear R (552/962), on the BW, up Went hill, joining a good track. After 0.3km bear R, DH, to a rd (West way), then bearing L on Lower street, then R on Upper street (nr Tiger Inn), to a T-J (557/ 979) in East dean. Turn L on the A259, UH, for 0.7km (0.45m), then R on Old Wilmington rd (Jevington) (550/982).

❽ After 0.25km (0.15m) bear R at a fork, for 0.4km (0.25m) then turn L (554/986), through a gate, on a BW, steep DH, to a rd. Turn R on this for 0.1km then turn L (552/988) on a BW (dirt track on the RHS of the drive). After 0.5km (0.3m), keep SA on a BW, into the trees, as the drive bears L, UH, across a field, into Friston forest.

❾ Follow this forest track (or the purple cycle trail, for a longer, more technical finish to the ride) for 1.3km (0.8m), through a clearing, SA over a path, up, then down some of Snap hill, to a X-tracks (544/005) and turn L.

❿ Follow this track (you came along at the start) for 2.25km (1.4m) (keeping R after 0.25km/0.15m), back to the houses in Westdean, and turn L on the BW, back to the car park (518/995).

EXTENSION 1:
+11.3KM (7M) & +310 metres climbing

❶ Keep SA/L, (Litlington), DH, through a farm, to a rd, (523/019), and turn L on it. After 0.5km (0.3m), through Litlington, after the rd bears R then L, turn R (522/016) on a BW (Frog Firle) opposite a thatched cottage. Go over a bridge, to a rd (517/019) by a YHA, and turn L on the rd.

❷ After 0.9km (0.55m), DH then UH, turn R, through a gate, on a grassy BW, into the trees (512/014). Keep L on the BW (R is a FP), UH, out of the trees, and turn R, over a field, following a fence on the RHS. Join a track, and follow this for 1.45km (0.9m) to a X-tracks (488/024), by a bench 'In loving memory of Paul Earle'.

❸ Turn R through a small gate, DH to a gate, then UH for 1.85km (1.15m) to a X-tracks (499/044), and turn R on the SDW. Follow the SDW for 2.9km (1.8m), DH, and keep SA on/as it joins Kings Ride rd (520/030) to T-J in Alfriston (520/030).

❹ Turn L on North street, going out of Alfriston, towards the A27 rd, for 0.65km (0.4m) then turn R over a bridge (522/036). To a T-J and go SA onto the SDW opposite, UH, for 0.7km (0.45m) to a rd (532/032). Keep SA, UH, on the SDW, and rejoin the main route at no. 3a.

SHORTCUT:
-14.2KM (8.8M) -395 metres of climbing

❶ Stay SA on the rd for another 0.1km and turn R on a BW (562/012), UH, for 0.9km (0.55m), into Friston forest. Keep SA on this BW forest track, DH, for 1km (0.65m) to a X-tracks (544/005) and go SA and rejoin route at no.10.

WAYMARKED ROUTES IN FRISTON FOREST

Ⓐ 11.3KM (7M), technical trail for experienced riders. Follow the purple markers around the forest.

There is also a 7.25KM (4.5M) easy route, for beginners and families. Follow the green markers, around the forest - ask at Cuckmere Cycles for a map.

GETTING THERE: This ride starts in Friston Forest at the National Trust (pay & display) car park (gets locked at dusk) (518/995). This is between Seaford and Eastbourne, on the A259 by a narrow bridge over Cuckmere river. There is also a good long stay car park (Willows) in Alfriston (522/033). There are railway stations in Seaford and Eastbourne (follow the A259 west).

ACCOMMODATION: B&B's at Exceat farmhouse on: 01323 870218, the George Inn on: 870319, Dean's barn on: 870319, The Giants Rest pub in Wilmington on: 870207, YHA in Alfriston on: 0870 8705666, Camping in Alfriston on: 01323 870560, or Sussex Ox (nr Alfriston) on: 870840, Eastbourne TI on: 01323 411400.

BIKE SHOPS: Cuckmere cycles, in the car park hire bikes tel: 01323870310or Evolution Cycles in Eastbourne on 01323 737320.

REFRESHMENTS: Cafe at Friston Forest VC, a pub just over the bridge, in Jevington, cafe at Birling gap, shops and pub in East Dean and Alfriston.

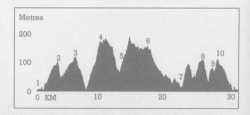

BEDGEBURY FOREST

FAMILY ROUTE

9KM (5.6M) family track

① An easy, well surfaced ride, suitable for all abilities.

SINGLETRACK ROUTE

13KM (8M) Intermediate trail

① A singletrack trail, that gets more challenging (and fun) the faster you go.

FREERIDE AREA

① North-shore (wooden constructions) riding for experienced riders only. Includes elevated ladder trails going up to about 2 metres, skinny balance logs (as thin as 4 inches wide), various drops, see-saws, wooden kickers, a three-way discombobulator (a set of linked see-saws), wooden bermed corners, and others. Next to the freeride area is a dirt jump area.

CYCLE SKILLS AREA

② An area set aside for cycle skills.

Facilities: There is cycle hire, purchase and repair (inlcuding bikes for the disabled), showers, bike wash, and cafe. There is also an adventure playground for non-cyclists.

TOP TIP: Bedgebury Cycle Club do social rides & trail maintenance. You will get an annual car parking pass, free showers and bike-wash, and discounts on parts and accessories in the Bedgebury bike shop. Visit www.boarsonbikes.co.uk for more info.

BEWL WATER

21KM (13M) 290 metres climbing

❶ **START.** Follow the 'Bewl water route' signs, heading west, for 1.2km (0.75m) to the lake and turn R (TQ 669/333).

❷ Follow the lake (on your LHS) for 5.1km (3.15m), then turn R through some gates (661/324) by a hut, following the BW sign. Short UH, to a DT and turn R on this, following the BW signs to a rd (665/322).

❸ Turn R on this rd, for 1km (0.6m) to a fork (663/314) and bear L, following the brown signs. 1.9km (1.2m) to a T-J (676/306) and turn L, on Burnt lodge lane.

❹ After 0.7km (0.45m), keep SA on Lower Hazlehurst, for 0.5km (0.3m) then through a 'Bewl water' gate (678/318). Follow the Bewl water signs for 5.3km (3.3m) alongside the water, to a T-J with a rd (700/318).

❺ Turn L, over the bridge, (or use the B2087 to Flimwell and include the Bedgebury loops) for 0.25km (0.15m) then turn L back onto the Bewl water track (700/320) and follow the signposts around Bewl water, for 5.2km (3.2m) back to the visitors centre (677/338).

GETTING THERE: The Bedgebury Forest route starts from the Visitors centre car park (715/337), off the B2079, and costs £6. There is a cafe, bike hire, bike wash, showers and a bike shop all on site here. The Bewl Water route starts from the Bewl Water Visitors centre car park (675/337), which is just off the A21 and can be found by following the brown signs, and costs £4.50 (at weekends, in season). Train station at Stonegate - head north, through Stonegate village, and over the B2099 rd to Bewl Water, by Ticehurst.

BIKE SHOPS: Evernden Cycles at the Visitors Centre in Bedgebury Forest, on 01580 879694 or see www.everndencycles.co.uk. and Bewl Water bike hire (summer only) on: 07801 670999.

ACCOMMODATION: B&B at the Cherry Tree Inn in Ticehurst on: 01580201229, B&B in Wadhurst on: 01892 783896, B&B in the 'Best Beach Inn' in Wadhurst, on: 01892 782046, Camping (on the north of Bewl water) off the A21, on: 01892 890566. Tunbridge wells TI on: 01892 515675 or www.heartofkent.org.uk

REFRESHMENTS: Bedgebury Forest has a cafe at the Pinetum centre (at the start / end of the family route) and Eugene's ice cream van. There are also showers and bike wash at the Bedgebury Forest Visitors Centre. Bewl Water has a cafe at the Bewl Water Visitors Centre.

35.3KM (22M) 665 metres of climbing

1 START. Go back to the A227 rd and go R on this, then L on a BW DT (TQ 632/614). To a rd and turn R on this, then L at a grass (623/613) on Platt house lane (Wrotham). 0.8km (0.5m) to a fork (620/606) and bear R on Rotham hill rd (Labour in vain), for 0.65km (0.4m) then go L towards Hilton park farm (private rd sign) (613/605).

2 After 0.7km (0.45m) go R through a green gate, on a BW (before a house) (612/598). DH, (with the M20 on the L below), to the bottom (606/599) and bear R, becoming a rd, to a fork (606/603) and bear R or see the extension.

3 After 1km (0.6km) turn L on a ByW (605/613), DH, to a rd and go SA (R then L) then R, back on the ByW (603/621). Follow this, to the corner of a rd (600/634) and go SA/R on this rd, past the pub into Ash, and turn R (no through rd) to Ash church & Manor (600/643).

4 Rough DT, DH, to a minor rd (612/645) and turn R on this, 0.8km (0.5m) to a T-J (611/638). Turn L, UH, then R on a BW to Hodsoll Street, keep SA/L on the rd, then turn L (627/627) to New Street. 1km (0.6m) to a X-roads (629/636) and go SA, then after 0.4km (0.25m) turn R by Keepers Cottage, (629/640), when the rd bears L.

5 Follow this track, L then R, DH, then UH to the A227 rd (638/648) and go R, then immediate L, on Steeles Lane. Turn R at the end of this, DH, on a ByW, out into a valley and keep SA at a X-tracks, onto Ridge Lane, and follow this rough rd, then bearing L on School Lane, DH, SA at X-tracks, UH, to a rd (648/627).

6 Turn L on the rd or see the shortcut, to a T-J in Harvel, by the pub, and turn R, past the village green, then L on a BW, then shortly R on the BW (653/632). Turn L at the T-J on tarmac, then very shortly R on a BW, DH, to a X-tracks (665/632). Turn L, for 0.65km (0.4m), then R on a ByW, steep UH, to a T-J at the top (669/634) and turn L (NDW).

7 Follow this rutted DT, ByW for 1.5km (0.95m) to a T-J (675/646) and turn R, under power lines, and keep R, alongside them, then turns L, fast DH, looking out for the R turn after 1km (0.6m) to Upper Halling (687/640). At the X-rds in Upper Halling (690/638) go R (Pilgrims Way), past a pub, keep SA after 0.65km (0.4m) on the 'Trackway'.

8 Keep SA on this trail, over a rd, and keep SA (changing track) for 1.45km (0.9m) to a fork (665/617) and go R UH, which then bears L (SP North Downs Way). Keep SA on this, becoming a DT by some houses, on the Pilgrims Way, for 3.15km (1.95m) to a rd (636/608).

9 Turn R on the rd, then shortly, go turn L on the Pilgrims Way ByW (635/608), (no SP), for 1.3km (0.8m), then turn R on a ByW (North Downs Way). Steep UH, to the A227 and go SA/R on this, over a X-rds, then shortly R, back to the visitor centre (633/610).

SHORTCUT

-10.1KM (6.3M) -215 metres of climbing

1 Turn R on the rd, then shortly L on a ByW, to X-rds and go SA on the rd, then keep SA on the ByW as the rd turns R, becoming steep DH, to the Pilgrims Way (652/612). Turn R on this DT, for 3.15km (1.95m) to a rd (636/608) and rejoin the route at no.9.

EXTENSION

+6KM (3.8M) & 145 metres climbing

1 Bear L (Labour in vain rd), for 1km (0.6m) (just past the elec. cables) then turn L to the A20 rd (597/605). Go SA onto a BW, through a gate, on a DT. Keep SA across the field, as the DT disappears, through a silver gate, over the M20, to a fork in the woods. BW is L, but there is some great ST if you bear R and choose a track bearing L, DH. You should end by a green barrier, by a rd, at the bottom (593/597), turn R on the rd.

*NOTE: If you turn R after 0.4km (0.25m), into the trees, you get back to the start of the DH runs.

2 After 0.55m, at a X-rds (587/602), turn R, under the M20, to the A20 (593/611). Turn R on this rd, for 0.5km (0.3m), then turn L and keep L on the rd, (north) towards Stansted and rejoin the route at no.3.

TROSLEY COUNTRY PARK

Cyclists are permitted to use the main routes through the woodland, if they are prepared to travel slowly and give way to pedestrians. There is a more challenging bridleway around the perimeter of the park if the main tracks are too tame for you.

GETTING THERE: Start from Trosley Country Park, visitors centre (GR 632/610). Exit the M20 at junction 2, on the A227 to Vigo Village and Trosley Country Park. Train station in Halling - head west on rd, 2km, UH, to Upper Halling.

ACCOMMODATION: B&B in Sevenoaks on: 01732 465262. B&B (Moorings Hotel) in Sevenoaks, on: 01732 452589. YHA in Kemsing (just north of the M26) on: 0870 7705890. Camping at Styants bottom (near Ingtham) on: 01732 762728. Sevenoaks TI on: 01732 450305.

BIKE SHOPS: Bikes, Bikes, Bikes in Sevenoaks on 01732 464997 / www.bikesbikesbikes.co.uk

REFRESHMENTS: Trosley Tea Room cafe at the start/end, sells snacks and hot & cold drinks (there is also a toilet here). On the route there are pubs at the X-rds near the start, another near junction 2 of the M20, Stansted, Ash, Hodsoll Street, Harvel, and Upper Halling.

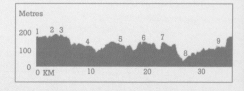

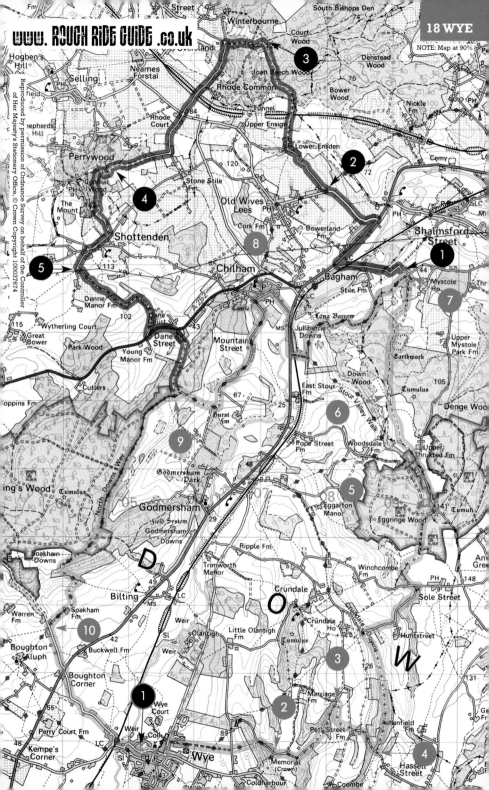

27.1KM (16.9M) 535 metres of climbing

❶ START. Back at the rd, turn R on this for 0.3km (0.2m) past the church and turn L on Olantigh rd (TR 055/468), for 0.25km (0.15m) then turn R on the (North Downs Way) BW (056/469). 1km (0.6m) to a rd and go SA, on a ST, UH through some woods to a rd (069/469).

❷ Turn R on the rd for 0.5km (0.3m) then go SA through a gate, as the track bears L, by the house. Go through another gate (075/467) and bear L for 1km (0.65m) along the edge of the woods, though a field, then DH, on a rocky track, to a T-J at the bottom (081/475).

❸ Turn sharp R, following the blue arrows, through a tunnel of trees, bearing L, for 0.55km (0.35m) to a drive. Go SA (between the hedges) on a ST, DH, to a DT and bear L, past a farm, UH on a DT, which bears R, for 0.4km (0.25m) and turn L at a metal gate (Kent CC sign) on a ByW (087/468) and follow this.

❹ 2km (1.25m) to a rd, (085/486) by a church, and go R on this for 1.2km (0.75m) DH then UH, to a T-J (094/493). Go L for 0.15km (0.1m) then R (FP) for 0.15km (0.1m) to a X-tracks (091/495) and go R and follow this main forest track for 1.2km (0.75m) to a rd (096/504).

❺ Go L on the rd for 0.8km (0.5m), past a factory on L, then keep SA on a BW, as the rd bears R (094/512). Keep SA inside the wood, on a ST as the DT goes R, keeping SA through the fields and gates, (cables overhead), for 1km (0.65m), to the edge of the wood (089/520), and bear to the L of them (not on the ST FP into them) (089/520).

❻ 0.3km (0.2m) and go through a gate and into the woods, following the blue BW arrows, DH, for 1.85km (1.15m) to a drive, by a farm. Turn L, to the corner of a rd (092/538) and turn immediately L on the (Stour valley walk) ByW or see the extension.

❼ Keep SA for 2.4km (1.5m) to a X-tracks by a wooden signpost (077/526), and turn R on the main track. DH, over the railway, to the A28 rd (074/526). Turn R on this for 0.65km (0.4m) then L on Branch rd, UH, for 0.4km (0.25m) to a T-J (071/536) and go L (towards the castle).

❽ To the square and bear L, then R (effectively SA) on Hambrook lane, to a T-J (069/534) and turn L (on Mountain street). After 1.7km (1.05m) keep SA on the ByW (NDW) (063/521), as the rd bears sharp L. Bearing R, UH, for 0.65km (0.4m), to the top (057/521), and turn L through a gate on the NDW.

❾ Follow the red arrows, on the NDW for 4.8km (3m), on a good track along the edge of Kings wood, through a farm, to a rd (038/486) and turn L on this.

❿ 0.7km (0.45m) to some off-set X-rds and go SA on Bramble lane (048/469) for 1.45km (0.9m) to a fork by the train station. Turn L, over the railway, and a bridge, then immediately turn L on Churchfield rd (049/469), and follow this rd back to the car park (052/468).

EXTENSION

+8.4KM (5.2M) 140 metres of climbing

❶ Go SA/L on the rd, DH, over a railway track, to the A28 rd (081/540). Turn R (use the path parallel to the rd) for 1km (0.6m) then turn L on Shalmsford rd (Old wives Lees) (088/546). After 1km (0.6m) on this rd, turn R at the fork (Lower Ensden).

❷ After 1km (0.6m) turn R on a BW, by a black barn (no sign) (074/556).After 0.7km (0.45m), just over a railway bridge, keep SA into the woods, on a ST BW (towards the Private sign) as the DT track bears R (074/564). Keep L at the fork on the BW to some X-tracks (070/572) at the edge of the woods.

❸ Turn L for 0.1m then bear R by a house, onto a DT and bear L, DH to a rd (064/572) and turn L on this for 1.3km (0.8m) to a X-rds (058/562). Go SA (Shottenden) for 0.65km (0.4m) then turn R on a rd (056/556). 0.4km (0.25m) to a fork and bear L for another 0.4km (0.25m) then turn L on the BW (048/554) (easy to miss).

❹ Through the trees and gates for 0.55km (0.35m) to a T-J (045/553) and turn L for another 0.65km (0.4m), then turn L on a ST, by a big tree (045/547). DH, joining a track and keep SA to a T-J with a rd (047/544) and turn R on the rd. Keep R for 0.4km (0.25m) to a X-rds (043/542) and turn L on Denne Manor lane (no through rd) for 0.3km (0.2m) then turn L on a ByW (042/539).

❺ Follow this for 1.85km (1.15m), DH to a rd (052/529) and turn L on this for 0.5km (0.3m), then turn R on Dane Street (ByW) by a house (057/530). 0.7km (0.45m) UH and bear L at the fork (057/521), for another 0.15km (0.1m) then turn R through a gate, on the NDW (057/521) and rejoin the main route at no.9.

GETTING THERE: This ride starts in the town of Wye in Kent. Exit the M20 at junction 9 and go north on the A28 (Canterbury) for just over 3 miles then turn R (Harville road) to Wye. Go over the railway and a bridge then turn left on Churchfield rd (after the 'The Tickled Trout' pub) and follow the parking signs to the (free) car park (052/468). Train station in Wye.

ACCOMMODATION: B&B's in Wye on: 01233 813011 and 813098, Woolpack B&B pub in Chilham on 01233 730208, YHA in Canterbury on 0870 770 5744. Camping at the Yew tree park on: 01227 700306 or Ashfield farm on: 01227 700624, Ashford TI on: 01233 629165, or Canterbury T.I. on: 01227 378100

BIKE SHOPS: Cycle Mart in Ashford on: 01233 622800

and in Canterbury on: 01227 761488 and Trev's cycles in Canterbury on: 01227 787880

REFRESHMENTS: Shop, pubs and toilets in Wye. On the route there pubs in Sole street, d pubs and tea shops in Chilham, and a shop in Bagham.

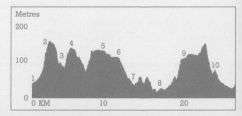

rough ride guide presents.....

Pictures provided by the Forestry Commission and Andy McCandlish.

man-made trails

Hundreds of way-marked, man-made trails in over 70 destinations in England, Scotland & Wales, providing thousands of miles of trails.

Also includes information on long distance / epic rides

available at www.roughrideguide.co.uk

rough ride guide presents.....

the maintenance & repair manual

Over 100 pages of step-by-step instructions with full colour pictures, for just about every job you are ever likely to do, from cleaning to changing the bottom bracket. This manual can also be updated as and when new components come out.

Saves you time & money

available at www.roughrideguide.co.uk

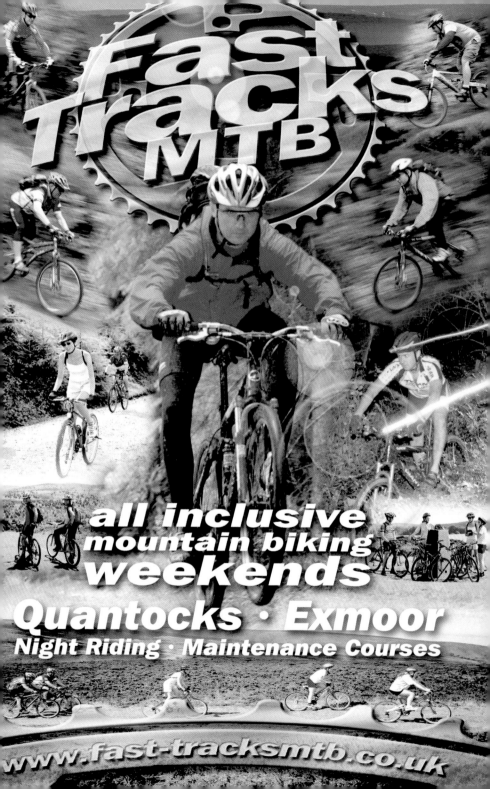

Wear it out.

sustrans
JOIN THE MOVEMENT

Sustrans is the UK's leading sustainable transport charity and is behind many groundbreaking projects including the 12,000 mile **National Cycle Network**.

Discover the Network with Sustrans' series of maps and guides to some of the UK's most breathtaking and challenging long distance rides.

For more information on the National Cycle Network, to buy maps and guides or to become a Sustrans Supporter visit or call:

www.sustrans.org.uk

0845 113 00 65

brought to you

by

ROUGH RiDE GUiDE